Emma Goss-Custard launched Honeybuns in 1998, in the city of Oxford. Emma and her husband Matt now run the award-winning bakery from Naish Farm in Dorset, where they continually develop new cakes and bakes with the help of their team. Their gluten-free cakes, brownies, traybakes and biscuits are sold in supermarkets, shops and cafes throughout the UK and into Europe, and are available from Honeybuns online shop: www.honeybuns.co.uk

Honeybuns

Honeybuns

Emma Goss-Custard

Honeybuns

gluten-free baking

PAVILION

This book is dedicated to Matt, Mal and Rak – for everything, my darlings

First published in the United Kingdom in 2012 by
PAVILION BOOKS
10 Southcombe Street
London
W14 0RA

An imprint of Anova Books Company Ltd

Commissioning editor: Becca Spry
Cover design & art direction: Georgina Hewitt
Designer: Miranda Harvey
Photographer: Cristian Barnett
Home economists: Charlotte Drake-Smith, Emma Marsden and Vicky Savage
Photography styling: Pene Parker, Emma Goss-Custard and Charlotte Drake-Smith
Editor: Maggie Ramsay
Proofreaders: Barbara Dixon, Matt Goss-Custard
Production: Laura Brodie

ISBN: 978-1-86205-947-4

A CIP catalogue record for this book is available from the British Library.

10 9 8 7 6 5 4 3 2 1

Repro by Mission Productions Ltd, Hong Kong
Printed by Toppan Leefung Printing Ltd, China

Notes
All of the recipes in this book use unsalted butter. We recommend using free-range eggs in all recipes. Recipes are based on large eggs unless otherwise stated. Duck eggs can be used for a richer result, but they are quite a bit bigger, so you may need to reduce the number.

Contents

The story of Honeybuns

Honeybuns Honeybuns started with just yours truly and an old Post Office bicycle in the beautiful city of Oxford. Necessity was the mother of invention. I was a scatty, over-anxious English graduate who, it's fair to say, was proving rather 'weak at interview'. Things were starting to look bleak as my contemporaries secured jobs and made their way in the world. I was beginning to wonder what the future might hold. Daydreaming through an English degree, I had been in my element. Real life revealed me as a hopeless romantic, ill-equipped for the cut and thrust of the real world. I was terrified.

Amidst all this self-doubt, I had happy memories of my student holiday jobs working in small bakeries. I'd also baked cakes throughout my studies. I couldn't type, but had set up a bartering system, exchanging lemon cakes for professionally presented essays. Would it be such a crazy idea to start my own cake delivery round? I had nothing to lose, and being able to look to my lifelong hobby of baking was, if not a 'eureka' moment, certainly a 'Doh! Why didn't I think of that sooner?' one.

Once I'd bought my bike and borrowed my gran's trusty old mixer I was off, wobbling but independent, and Honeybuns was born. I was lucky to have been given some lovely recipes by my gran, who had been influenced by Northern Italian baking. They featured indigenous ingredients, including polenta, ground almonds and ground hazelnuts, and were naturally light on wheat flour. I realized quite quickly that, with careful modification, the wheat flour and 'hidden' gluten present in other ingredients could be avoided altogether. The resulting cakes tasted gorgeous and were naturally gluten-free.

After a couple of years of baking in a chaotic, shared student house, I moved to Guildford, where my future husband was working. The move gave me additional markets to grow into, and I could easily hop on the train to London to present to buyers. By this time there were 5 of us at Honeybuns doing everything from baking to packing to delivering. An ongoing order for Spicy cat cookies (see page 132) for Virgin Trains resulted in hectic days, but helped us to afford a bigger oven and ultimately the move to Dorset. So thank you Sir Richard Branson – you helped us take the plunge and get a little more business-minded.

We moved to Naish Farm in Dorset in 2002 to get closer to nature, our suppliers and the rural life we wanted. Over the last 10 years, the old dairy farm has been gently adapted and converted to a house the bakery. Today, Honeybuns employs 25 people and supplies cakes, cookies and other baked goodies to shops, cafés and online customers throughout the UK and abroad. Naish Farm is also home to our collection of rescue animals and pets, and is surrounded by our nature reserve. Our charming Bee Shack café is housed in one of the old chicken sheds, and has become a bit of a cult hit. This is possibly the least commercial café in the UK – it's open to visitors just once a month. But it gives us a great opportunity to get some face-to-face feedback on new flavour combinations. Our customers soon let us know if we've lost the culinary plot. We also eat together as a team in the café 3 times a week. We try out new recipes, and if it doesn't taste amazing, it's back to the mixing bowl. My feeling is that this non-laboratory approach is what keeps Honeybuns products genuine.

We have many archived recipes, and it's a pleasure to share some of them via this book. There are recipes that we enjoy in our Bee Shack café too. We also wanted to do our bit to demystify gluten-free baking. The recipes are generally easy to follow: we're definitely of the 'pop it in a single bowl and mix' school of baking.

It is true that baking is more exact than other methods of cooking, but there is still much scope for adventure, fun and experimentation. With any baking recipe, even if you follow it to the letter, you will come up against such variables as egg sizes, the moisture content of your butter, humidity levels, and the mood of your oven on the day. In other words, every baking recipe, gluten-free or not, will have your own unique interpretation, conscious or otherwise. In our view any mistakes may result in a delicious new invention.

Our cakes are intended to be indulgent treats, using the very best of ingredients and celebrating Mother Nature, seasonality and artisan food production. They just happen to be gluten-free, too.

Our recipes are biased towards the rustic. Your sugar-craft skills will not be called on. We love taking inspiration from what can be found in the garden or window box. Far better to use up whatever soft fruits you have around than to go out and buy strawberries for the Strawberry cobbler (see page 150) – blueberries, loganberries, raspberries or blackberries would do just as well and you will feel all the more creative.

Please don't be deterred by the occasional long ingredients list. Once you have got your storecupboard stocked and have explored a few recipes, you'll soon be comfortably cooking gluten-free. If you have fun choosing when you want to follow the recipes and when you'd prefer to go creatively solo, then we will be happy. We'll be over-the-moon-happy if you enjoy eating the results.

We'd love to hear your thoughts and comments on our recipes. Please email us at thebee@honeybuns.co.uk or post a comment on:
www.facebook.com/HoneybunsBakery
www.twitter.com/HoneybunsBakery
www.youtube.com/HoneybunsBakery

We really hope you enjoy baking with Honeybuns.

Emma Goss-Custard

Gluten-free baking

At Honeybuns we believe gluten-free cooking can be exciting and creative, and the results utterly gorgeous. Just like any other cooking, in fact. Some of the ingredients in this book may sound strange at first, but once you get to know them you'll be able to take our recipes and run with them.

Over the years we have road-tested lots of combinations of ingredients and learnt which work best for us. Our recipe development is a continual process as there are new foods coming onto the market all the time.

We always focus on what can be done – brilliantly – with the resources available. We don't worry about being able to 'translate' traditional recipes to gluten-free precisely... down this path disappointment and vexation lie. For example, what baking book would be complete without a scone recipe? A traditional wheat-flour scone would contain milk. Instead, our recipe (see page 45) uses ground almonds and almond oil. Not a purist's approach, but it results in an amazingly light texture and the scones keep well for up to 3 days.

Buying ingredients

Thank goodness for the internet. There are numerous online purveyors of gluten-free ingredients that would otherwise be tricky to track down. Specialist importers offer gluten-free essentials such as tapioca and sorghum flours. Until recently, some of our favoured ingredients were only available to 'trade', but online suppliers increasingly offer 'professional' brands to everyone. It sometimes means having to order slightly bigger amounts than you'd like to – but many ingredients can be frozen. We have listed a number of our tried-and-tested suppliers on page 170-173. Supermarkets have also expanded their 'free from' ranges in recent years. Independent delis, farm shops and health food shops remain great places to seek out ingredients and specialist knowledge.

Gluten-free ingredients

We often use polenta, and toasted and ground nuts such as almonds, pistachios and hazelnuts. We've taken inspiration from northern Italy, where these ingredients are commonly used. Ground nuts have a softer texture and higher moisture content than rice flours and typical gluten-free flour mixes. We sometimes use rice flour, but only in combination with other flours. We need our cakes to last longer than just a day or two wherever possible, and the natural oiliness of ground nuts helps keep them moist.

We are mindful, however, that nut prices have risen dramatically in recent years. Ground flax seed (linseed) is less expensive and can be used to replace some or all of the nuts. Flax has a naturally nutty flavour and a sweetness, and behaves in much the same way as ground almonds in cooking.

Sorghum flour and tapioca flour are soft and absorbent, resulting in light, fluffy cakes. We steer clear of potato-derived flours as they can be heavy, and we use chickpea flour (gram flour) sparingly as it can have a slightly sour taste. Gluten-free oats and oat flour are great for adding texture, but check that they are certified gluten-free, as this is not always the case.

For binding and thickening we prefer guar gum to xanthan gum. Guar gum is a wholly natural product made from a type of bean, while xanthan gum is corn-based and more highly processed. It can result in a slightly heavier texture in some recipes.

Nuts and seeds

Many of the recipes in this book call for nuts or seeds, which are used whole, chopped or ground. We recommend buying whole nuts in their skins for most recipes, but ready-ground nuts are usually more finely ground than they can be in a food processor, which results in a lighter-textured cake. If you are grinding your own nuts you can toast them first to add flavour.

To toast nuts, coconut chips or seeds, preheat the oven to 180°C/350°F/Gas 4. Spread the nuts or seeds out on a baking sheet and toast in the oven for 5 minutes. If any are slightly overdone or blackened, discard them as they will taste bitter.

Leave the nuts to cool, and then chop or grind them as required. We use the following terms:

- **roughly chopped** – use a knife or give a brief burst in a food processor to chop the nuts into pieces about 1–2 cm/½–¾ in
- **chopped** – use a knife or give a brief burst in a food processor to chop the nuts into pieces about the size of dried lentils (about 5 mm/¼ in)
- **ground** – blitz the nuts in a food processor until the pieces are as fine as you can make them, like fine breadcrumbs

If you want to keep a stock of toasted nuts, freezing them is a great way to preserve freshness and flavour.

Adapting recipes

We hope you will be inspired to cook our recipes again and again, making changes to suit your tastes and using fruits and vegetables that are in season. If you are going to adapt a recipe, it is wise to swap one ingredient at a time. A lot of our chosen flours and ground nuts are interchangeable.

You will also see how we adapt mixtures for different uses: for example, the shortbread that you make and then chill and roll out thinly for the little Iced gems (see page 140) is also used as the base for Strawberry cobbler (see page 150). With a bit of tweaking – perhaps by adding an egg – this dough could become a more versatile pastry.

Plenty of delicious new products have been born of 'mistakes' in our test kitchen. I've forgotten to pop eggs in a muffin mixture on more than one occasion. The resulting 'muffettes' can happily be frozen and then used in a trifle (see page 147) or sweet tian (see page 160). Similarly, you can make gluten-free crumbs from any spare cookies, cakes or muffins. Crumbs can be frozen and then toasted for sprinkling over baked fruits or trifles.

Tips and techniques

Gluten lends stretch and 'glue' to a mixture. In certain cake recipes, the lack of gluten is not so critical. For example, you can achieve a wonderfully textured brownie using ground almonds in place of wheat flour. Pastry, however, is more of a challenge to create without gluten (see the notes on pastry, opposite).

When making cakes, brownies and other beaten mixtures, ensure your ingredients are at room temperature and not straight from the fridge. If you add anything too hot or too cold it can cause the mixture to shrink during cooking.

If your mixture includes beaten eggs, be careful not to pour warm melted butter or chocolate directly onto the eggs, as the heat may cause them to scramble.

If baking powder comes into contact with anything acidic, it may react and cause the mixture to separate, so it's a good idea to keep it insulated from acidic ingredients such as lemon or orange juice, zest or oil, rhubarb or other acidic fruit. When adding ingredients to a mixing bowl, always 'sandwich' the baking powder between other dry ingredients, such as flours or sugar.

Pastry

In our experience, pastry dough without gluten requires a little TLC. For instance, the pastry used in the Blackcurrant flummery pie on page 158 is quite prone to breaking up. This is not an issue as long as you are happy to use your fingers to squidge the pastry into shape. Each of our pastry recipes can bear a little hand-moulding – but it's best to work quickly and run your hands under cold water to avoid getting the pastry too warm.

All of our pastries are easier to handle if chilled for an hour or so before rolling out. Using a liberal dusting of tapioca flour and rolling pastry mixes between sheets of silicone paper are nifty tricks. With butter-based pastries and crusts you need to work with chilled and cubed or grated butter.

In warmer weather you'll often end up with a stickier dough and in colder weather you may need to mix it for longer and hand-mould it into something workable. You just need the confidence to manually handle it and swiftly squidge it into shape.

Sometimes you may need to add a little milk or egg yolk as a binder; this is detailed in each pastry recipe where relevant. Pastry is more vulnerable to variables than other forms of baking: room temperature, moisture levels and your body temperature all have an effect. Once you've made the mixtures a couple of times you'll get a feel for what to adjust.

Sometimes the recipe asks you to bake the pastry blind; this works well without a need for baking beans or parchment paper. We aim to keep things simple where there is no adverse effect on taste or texture.

Cinnamon sugar, vanilla sugar

For cinnamon sugar, mix ground cinnamon with an equal weight of light brown sugar and pour it into a dredger. This can be made ahead of time and stored in the larder, but only make up a small amount as the flavour of ground cinnamon (and all ground spices) diminishes quickly. We keep ground spices in sealed sandwich bags in the freezer to prolong their life.

For vanilla sugar, fill a 500 g or 1 lb kilner jar with granulated sugar (or light brown sugar) and add 2 vanilla pods. It'll take a couple of weeks for the vanilla flavour to infuse the sugar, after which you can decant it into a dredger or sprinkle it from the jar.

Melting chocolate

Many of the recipes require melted butter, melted chocolate, or a mixture of both of these. We suggest using either a bain-marie or microwave to melt chocolate. The microwave has speed and convenience in its favour, but you have to be a little more careful not to overheat the mixture.

Chocolate should be chopped into roughly equal-sized chunks, for even melting. Chocolate 'callets' (chocolate drops) are an alternative used by professional cooks and increasingly available to the domestic cook (see page 170).

We usually melt chocolate with either butter or oil. This gives a gloss to the chocolate and makes the melted mixture smoother and more spreadable. It also results in a softer set chocolate, so if you are making a chocolate coating and want a more brittle set, melt the chocolate on its own.

- **Microwave** – use a low power setting until you are familiar with how long your microwave takes to melt without overheating. After that you can use medium or high power for melting larger quantities. Make sure the bowl and spoon are dry, as any moisture can cause melted chocolate to go grainy and there's no guaranteed way to reverse this. A metal spoon or rubber spatula are better than a wooden spoon, as it's easier to be sure they are completely dry. Also, make sure the bowl is microwaveable and won't overheat. When melting the ingredients, check every 30 seconds and stir to ensure even melting. With practice, you will get used to mixtures that can be left a little longer between stirs. White chocolate burns particularly easily, so take extra care with this.

- **Bain-marie** – Place the ingredients to be melted in a heatproof glass bowl. Using a saucepan that is slightly smaller than the bowl, pour in water to a depth of 2 cm/¾ in and bring to simmering point. Place the bowl on top of the saucepan; the bowl should rest on the pan without coming into contact with the water. Simmer, but be sure not to allow water or steam to come into contact with the mixture. Stir with a rubber spatula. Remove from the heat just before it is fully melted and then stir until it is evenly melted – this helps avoid overheating the mixture.

Zesting and juicing citrus fruit

To zest fruit, we use a fine hand-held grater. The fruit can then be cut in half and juiced with a hand juicer. Recipes usually call for the juice of 1 or 2 fruit; larger quantities are listed in ml/fl oz, so you can measure from a carton of fresh juice. If you've zested a lemon or orange but don't need the juice, the fruit can be frozen for use in another recipe.

Equipment

All baking must be done in a preheated oven. The oven temperature and baking times are given in each recipe. Many of our recipes begin by lining the baking tin with baking parchment – it's fantastic stuff and allows your cakes, cookies and pastries to slide easily out of their tins. It is also sold as silicone paper or non-stick baking paper. Pre-shaped silicone paper loaf tin and cake tin liners in various sizes are available from specialist cookware shops or online (try www.lakeland.co.uk).

Where the recipe mentions a food processor, a hand-held blender is an alternative, particularly when working with small quantities. Some types of baking tins must always be put into the oven on a rigid metal baking tray for safety. These are:

- loose-bottomed tart tins
- springform tins
- bendy silicone muffin pans and individual bun/cake cases

When making muffins and small cakes, we use either paper cake cases in a rigid muffin tin, or a bendy silicone muffin pan. The choice depends on how sticky the baked muffins are (silicone is best for sticky) and whether we want the muffins to be more portable (when paper cases are best).

When icing and decorating cakes, we use a lazy susan – a rotating turntable that makes it easy to turn the cake as you ice.

cakes

Honeybuns

Gooseberry fool cake

150 g/5½ oz/⅔ cup butter, melted, plus extra for brushing
tapioca flour, for dusting
5 eggs
200 g/7 oz/1 cup light brown sugar
200 g/7 oz/2 cups ground almonds
100 g/3½ oz sorghum flour
1½ tsp gluten-free baking powder
1½ tsp guar gum
1 tsp vanilla extract
pinch of salt
450 g/1 lb green gooseberries, topped, tailed, rinsed and dried

FROSTED BERRIES

7 whole gooseberries, topped, tailed, rinsed and dried
1 tbsp pasteurized liquid egg white
1–2 tbsp caster (superfine) sugar

ELDERFLOWER CREAM

200 ml/7 fl oz double (heavy) cream
2 tbsp elderflower cordial
40 g/1½ oz/⅓ cup icing (confectioners') sugar, sifted

makes: 1 x 23 cm/9 in round cake
health: gluten-free
cook: 45 minutes
store: 3 days in fridge. Freezes well without the icing
compost: eggshells, gooseberry trimmings

This gooseberry-laden sponge marries brilliantly with the light-as-a-feather elderflower topping. Its high fruit content means that it's a good source of vitamins A and C. This cake is best made with the really tart, early season green gooseberries. You can use red or yellow varieties, but they are quite a lot sweeter. If fresh gooseberries are hard to find, you can use frozen ones. As it is so moist, this cake needs to be kept in the fridge. The icing will wilt after a day or 2 simply re fluff it with a fork.

Preheat the oven to 180°C/350°F/Gas 4. Line a 23 cm/9 in round springform tin with a disc of baking parchment, then brush with melted butter and dust with tapioca flour.

Crack the eggs into a large mixing bowl and beat with an electric mixer on high speed. Add the melted butter and beat again. Add the sugar, almonds, sorghum flour, baking powder, guar gum, vanilla and salt, then beat until creamy. Stir in the gooseberries using a rubber spatula. Be gentle: you want to keep them intact.

Spoon the mixture into the tin and bang the tin firmly on a work surface to get rid of air pockets. Bake for 45 minutes, until firm and springy to the touch. A flat cake skewer will come out clean when the cake is ready.

Leave the cake in its tin for 10–15 minutes, then turn it out, right way up, onto a rack covered with baking parchment. Leave to cool , then peel off the parchment.

For the frosted berries, wash the gooseberries and pat them dry. Brush them lightly with egg white, then roll them in caster sugar. Place the coated berries on a piece of baking parchment and leave to dry.

For the elderflower cream topping, whisk the cream with the cordial and icing sugar until it forms stiff peaks. Spread the cream over the cake with a palette knife: we like a rough peaked finish, but you could go super sleek. Decorate with the frosted berries.

Make the most of your freezer

If you have a glut of gooseberries, make a batch of cakes and freeze them; apply the icing after they've thawed.

Bumble Barrow fruit cake

makes: 1 x 18 cm/7 in round cake
health: gluten-free
cook: 60–70 minutes
store: 7 days in airtight tin, freezes well
compost: eggshells, tea bags, orange

1 good-quality tea bag
50 g/1¾ oz/5 tbsp plump raisins
50 g/1¾ oz natural colour glacé (candied) cherries, chopped
40 g/1½ oz soft dried apricots, chopped
175 g/6 oz/¾ cup butter, plus extra, melted, for brushing
tapioca flour, for dusting
grated zest and juice of 1 orange
½ tsp orange oil
100 g/3½ oz Amondi cookies (see page 130)
25 g/1 oz stem ginger in syrup (drained weight)
2 eggs
150 g/5½ oz/¾ cup light brown sugar, plus 1 tbsp for topping
100 g/3½ oz/generous ½ cup glutinous rice flour
1 tsp gluten-free baking powder
100 g/3½ oz/1 cup walnuts, toasted, ground
50 g/1¾ oz/scant ½ cup polenta
50 g/1¾ oz/⅓ cup almonds, toasted, chopped
25 g/1 oz good-quality mixed (candied) peel
½ tsp mixed spice
1 tsp vanilla extract

This name is a play on words in honour of an amazing corner of Dorset properly known as Bulbarrow Hill. We can see Bulbarrow from our café windows and we've had many a happy hike up to the top. This robust yet moist cake was dreamt up with such adventures in mind. Soaking the fruit in tea adds even more moisture and depth of flavour. I'd also suggest trying a slice of this with a chunk of proper farmhouse Cheddar.

The day before you plan to make your cake, soak the fruit. Pour 100 ml/3½ fl oz boiling water over the tea bag, then leave to cool for 30 minutes. Put the raisins, cherries and apricots into a bowl, pour over the tea (with the tea bag), cover and leave overnight.

Preheat the oven to 170°C/325°F/Gas 3. Line an 18 cm/7 in round springform tin with a disc of baking parchment, then brush with melted butter and dust with tapioca flour. Melt the butter with the orange zest; leave to cool slightly, then add the orange oil. Strain the tea-soaked fruit, discarding the tea bag. Whizz the Amondi cookies to crumbs in a food processor or blender. Crush the ginger using a food processor or blender.

Crack the eggs into a large mixing bowl. Add all of the remaining ingredients, including the orange juice, crushed ginger, crushed cookies and strained fruit, adding the butter mixture last. Beat thoroughly with an electric mixer until the mixture is smooth and pale orange.

Spoon the mixture into the tin and bang the tin firmly on a work surface to get rid of air pockets. Bake for 35 minutes, then cover with a piece of baking parchment to prevent it from burning. Bake for a further 30–35 minutes, until firm to the touch. A flat cake skewer will come out clean when the cake is ready. Sprinkle the cake with 1 tbsp light brown sugar. Leave to cool in the tin.

For extra 'ooh-la-la'

For a richer flavour, replace the light brown sugar with muscovado. Double up the recipe and bake in a 23 cm/9 in tin for a very special Christmas cake.

Toffee-topped almond and rhubarb cake

225 g/8 oz/1 cup butter, melted, plus extra for brushing
3 eggs
140 g/5 oz/1½ cups ground almonds
70 g/2½ oz/generous ½ cup polenta
70 g/2½ oz sorghum flour
1 tsp gluten-free baking powder
140 g/5 oz/scant ¾ cup light brown sugar
140 g/5 oz/1 cup almonds, toasted, chopped
1 tsp almond extract
½ tsp vanilla extract

ROASTED RHUBARB

300 g/10½ oz rhubarb, cut into 4–5 cm/1½ –2 in chunks
70 g/2½ oz/⅓ cup light brown sugar
3 tbsp amaretto

TOFFEE RHUBARB

75 g/2¾ oz/5 tbsp butter
70 g/2½ oz/⅓ cup light brown sugar
½ tbsp golden syrup
100 g/3½ oz rhubarb, cut into 4–5 cm/1½ –2 in chunks

ALMOND PRALINE TOPPING

55 g/2 oz/scant ½ cup almonds
90 g/3¼ oz/½ cup granulated sugar

makes: 1 x 23 cm/9 in round cake
health: gluten-free
cook: about 1 hour
store: 3 days in fridge
compost: eggshells, rhubarb

As well as looking great, this cake delivers on taste and texture and is arguably good for you! Rhubarb is a great source of vitamins A and C. This is equally delicious served warm with clotted cream or crème fraîche.

Preheat the oven to 180°C/350°F/Gas 4. Line a 23 cm/9 in round springform tin with a disc of baking parchment, then brush with melted butter and dust with tapioca flour. To roast the rhubarb, place it in a roasting tin, sprinkle with the sugar and amaretto and bake for about 20 minutes, stirring halfway through. You want the rhubarb to keep its shape. Remove from the oven and allow to cool.

For the toffee rhubarb, put the butter in a pan and melt over a medium–low heat, then add the sugar, golden syrup and rhubarb. Stir gently with a wooden spoon until a toffee sauce forms. Turn the heat down and simmer for 5–7 minutes, or until the rhubarb is tender, but not too broken up. Set aside. Turn the oven down to 170°C/325°F/Gas 3.

Crack the eggs into a large mixing bowl. Add all the dry ingredients and a pinch of salt, then add the almond and vanilla extracts, melted butter, toffee rhubarb and 100 g/3½ oz of the roasted rhubarb. Beat with an electric mixer at medium speed until combined and creamy. Pour the mixture into the tin. Bake for 30 minutes, then cover with a piece of baking parchment and bake for a further 10–12 minutes, or until springy to the touch and a flat cake skewer comes out clean.

Leave the cake to cool in the tin for 1 hour. Turn out, peel off the baking parchment and slide the cake onto a serving plate. Spoon the remaining roasted rhubarb evenly over the top of the cake, along with any cooking syrup. (The syrup may need reheating to be pourable.) To make the almond praline topping, roughly chop the almonds and put them and the sugar in a small saucepan over a low heat. Stir continuously until the sugar has completely dissolved and formed a golden liquid coating the almonds; take care as this liquid is very hot. Drizzle the praline over the rhubarb. Allow to cool and set before attempting to eat!

Make the most of your freezer

If you have a glut of rhubarb, roast it as above, with water instead of amaretto if you like, then cool and freeze to use in crumbles and pies.

Raspberry and white chocolate cake

makes: 1 x 20 cm/8 in round cake
health: gluten-free
cook: 40–45 minutes
store: eat on same day
compost: eggshells

melted butter, for brushing
tapioca flour, for dusting
4 eggs
150 g/5½ oz/¾ cup light brown sugar
125 g/4½ oz/1¾ cups hazelnuts, ground
50 g/1¾ oz/scant ½ cup polenta
25 g/1 oz sorghum flour
1½ tsp gluten-free baking powder
1½ tsp guar gum
75 g/2¾ oz/generous 1 cup hazelnuts, toasted and chopped
150 g/5½ oz white chocolate, chopped
5–6 tbsp top-quality raspberry jam, for filling
24 raspberries, to decorate

ROASTED RASPBERRIES

200 g/7 oz raspberries
4 tbsp clear honey
½ tsp cinnamon sugar

CREAM FILLING AND TOPPING

200 g/7 oz mascarpone
100 ml/3½ fl oz/⅓ cup double (heavy) cream
100 g/3½ oz crème fraîche
60 g/2¼ oz/½ cup icing (confectioners') sugar
2 tsp lemon juice and 1 tsp vanilla extract

RASPBERRY SUGAR

1 freeze-dried raspberry
1 tsp icing (confectioners') sugar

This is simple to make, perfect for a summer's day. Once the topping is on, the cake should be quickly admired and then eaten before the cream slides off.

Preheat the oven to 180°C/350°F/Gas 4. Brush 2 x 20 cm/8 in round shallow cake tins with melted butter and dust with tapioca flour.

For the roasted raspberries, put the berries in a baking tin, drizzle the honey over them and dredge with cinnamon sugar. Roast in the oven for 20 minutes. Leave to cool for 5 minutes.

Crack the eggs into a large mixing bowl, then add the sugar, ground hazelnuts, polenta, sorghum flour, baking powder, guar gum and ¼ tsp salt. Beat with an electric mixer until creamy and stiff. Using a rubber spatula, gently stir in the chopped nuts, white chocolate and roasted raspberries.

Divide the mixture between the tins. Bake for 20–25 minutes, until a flat cake skewer comes out clean. Leave the cakes in the tins for a couple of minutes, then turn out onto a rack. Invert one so its flat bottom side is upwards.

For the cream filling, put the mascarpone, cream, crème fraîche, icing sugar, lemon juice and vanilla into a bowl and beat with an electric mixer until stiff.

For the raspberry sugar, use the back of a spoon to crush the freeze-dried raspberry to a fine powder. Sift in the 1 tsp icing sugar – if it is not pink enough, add a little more raspberry. Only mix little by little as you need it, as the freeze-dried raspberry goes soft after a couple of hours.

Spread 1 cake thickly with raspberry jam. Spread half the cream filling on top of the jam and place the second cake on top. Spread the remaining cream filling on top of the cake. Arrange the raspberries on top and dust the cake with raspberry sugar.

Give it a twist

You can use any soft summer berries for this cake.

Upside-down polenta plum cake

makes: 1 x 900 g/2 lb loaf cake
health: gluten-free
cook: 45–50 minutes
store: best eaten on same day. Freezes well
compost: eggshells, plum trimmings, orange skins

100 g/3½ oz/scant ½ cup butter, melted, plus extra for brushing
2 eggs
185 g/6½ oz/1½ cups polenta
60 g/2¼ oz/⅔ cup ground almonds
1½ tsp gluten-free baking powder
¾ tsp guar gum
¾ tsp vanilla extract
185 g/6½ oz rice syrup
200 g/7 oz crème fraîche
2 tbsp orange juice

TOPPING

8 red plums, halved and pitted
4 tbsp light brown sugar
100 ml/3½ fl oz/⅓ cup orange juice

This is a great cake for using up any bumper seasonal fruit harvests. Instead of plums you could use damsons or peaches – or any fruit with a bit of body. The great thing about red-skinned plums (we use Victoria plums) is that you benefit from the gorgeous colour contrast against the sunshine yellow of the polenta. The cake itself is not very sweet, but when it is turned upside down those lovely syrupy fruit juices seep into the sponge. Delicious served warm with home-made custard (see page 147).

Preheat the oven to 180°C/350°F/Gas 4. Brush a 900 g/2 lb loaf tin with melted butter, line with a silicone loaf tin liner, then liberally butter the loaf liner.

First, make the topping. Put the plums, skin side up, in a baking tin. Mix the brown sugar and orange juice and pour over the plums. Roast in the oven for 15–17 minutes, until soft but still keeping their shape. Leave to cool in the tin.

Crack the eggs into a large mixing bowl, then add the polenta, almonds, baking powder, guar gum and vanilla extract. In another bowl, mix the melted butter with the rice syrup, crème fraîche and orange juice. Beat with an electric mixer at low speed until just combined. Don't worry if it looks a bit curdled. Pour this mixture over the dry ingredients and beat at high speed until smooth and pale.

Take the plums out of the tin and put them in the loaf tin, skin side down. Pour the syrup that remains in the baking tin into a measuring jug and pour 20 ml/4 tsp of the syrup over the plums in the loaf tin. Reserve the rest.

Spoon the cake mixture into the loaf tin and spread it gently. Bake for 30 minutes, then cover with a disc of baking parchment and bake for a further 15–20 minutes, until springy to the touch; a flat cake skewer will come out clean when the cake is ready. As soon as the cake comes out of the oven, loosen the sides with a knife, then place a serving plate upside down on top of the tin and turn over quickly. Remove the tin and peel off the baking parchment. Spoon the remaining syrup from cooking the plums over the cake while it is still warm.

Dorset apple cake

275 g/9¾ oz/generous 1 cup butter, melted, plus extra for brushing
tapioca flour, for dusting
200 g/7 oz/1¼ cups raisins
2 tbsp Somerset cider brandy, Calvados or brandy
250 g/9¾ oz dessert apples
juice of 1 lemon
3 eggs
300 g/10½ oz/1½ cups vanilla granulated sugar
250 g/9 oz/2½ cups ground almonds
70 g/2½ oz millet flour
60 g/2¼ oz glutinous rice flour
2 tsp gluten-free baking powder
1 tsp guar gum
1 tsp ground cinnamon

TOPPING

2 dessert apples, thinly slices
1 tbsp cinnamon sugar

makes: 1 x 23 cm/9 in round cake
health: gluten-free
cook: 60–70 minutes
store: 5 days in fridge. Freezes well
compost: apple cores, eggshells, lemon skins

We are lucky to have a few traditional apple trees here at Naish Farm. Many Dorset orchards have disappeared, but there is keen interest in reinstating them. There are some fabulously named local apple varieties such as Slack ma Girdle and Buttery Door. This recipe comes into its own as the mellow mists of September descend. We mop up any spare dessert apples – it doesn't matter which variety – and add them to the mix. With the Somerset Cider Brandy Company on our doorstep, we felt it would be churlish not to add a splash or two of their award-winning cider brandy.

Preheat the oven to 170°C/325°F/Gas 3. Line a 23 cm/9 in round cake tin with a disc of baking parchment, then brush with melted butter and dust with tapioca flour. Put the raisins in a small saucepan, add the cider brandy and heat gently for 2 minutes. Set aside.

Core and peel the apples. Cut them into 2–3 cm/1 in cubes, place in a bowl and toss in the lemon juice. Set aside.

Crack the eggs into a large mixing bowl, then add all of the dry ingredients, together with the raisins and brandy. Pour in the melted butter. Beat with an electric mixer until you have a smooth, pale batter. Then, using a rubber spatula, stir in the apples. Make sure the cinnamon is evenly mixed.

Spoon the mixture into the prepared tin and spread evenly. Bang the tin firmly on a work surface to get rid of air pockets. Decorate the top of the cake with thin slices of apple, pushing them into the mixture in a spiral pattern so that just the skin is showing. Sprinkle with the cinnamon sugar.

Bake for 20 minutes, then cover with baking parchment to prevent the topping from burning. Bake for a further 40–50 minutes, or until the surface springs back when pressed gently with your fingertips. A flat cake skewer will come out moist but clean when the cake is ready. (The cooking time will vary quite a lot depending on the moisture content of your apples; after an hour, check every 10 minutes.) Leave to cool in the tin; turn out when cold, then peel off the parchment.

Great for kids

To make a non-alcoholic version, replace the brandy with apple juice.

Banana cake

makes: 1 x 450 g/1 lb loaf cake
health: gluten-free
cook: 40 minutes
store: 5 days in fridge. Freezes well
compost: banana skins, eggshells

75 g/2¾ oz/5 tbsp butter, melted, plus extra for brushing
tapioca flour, for dusting
2 eggs
100 g/3½ oz/½ cup light brown sugar
100 g/3½ oz/1 cup ground almonds
50 g/1¾ oz/5 tbsp ground brown flax seeds (linseed)
1 tsp ground cinnamon
¾ tsp guar gum
¾ tsp gluten-free baking powder
pinch of salt
325 g/11½ oz bananas (about 3 medium bananas)
70 g/2½ oz/scant ½ cup raisins
25 g/1 oz sunflower seeds, toasted

TOPPING
1 banana
about 1 tbsp cinnamon sugar

This has a stupendously high fruit content. You could add chocolate chunks to the mixture too, but we love the unadulterated banana hit. The moistness is off the scale!

Preheat the oven to 170°C/325°F/Gas 3. Line a 450 g/1 lb loaf tin with baking parchment, then brush with melted butter and dust with tapioca flour.

Break the eggs into a large mixing bowl, then add the sugar, almonds, flax seeds, cinnamon, guar gum, baking powder and salt. Add the melted butter and, using an electric mixer, beat at high speed until smooth and fairly runny.

Break the bananas into bite-sized chunks, then add them, the raisins and seeds to the bowl and stir gently with a rubber spatula. The ingredients should be well mixed, but keep the banana pieces intact.

Spoon the mixture into the tin and bang the tin firmly on a work surface to get rid of air pockets. For the topping, cut the banana into slices 3 mm/⅛ in thick and place in an overlapping line on top of the cake. Sprinkle with cinnamon sugar.

Bake for 35 minutes, then cover with baking parchment and bake for a further 5 minutes or until firm to the touch and a flat cake skewer comes out clean and just slightly moist. Do not open the oven door too often or the cake may sink. It will rise nicely but might sink a bit as it cools. Leave to cool completely before you take it out of its tin and peel off the baking parchment.

For extra 'ooh-la-la'

This cake can be gently warmed and served with home-made custard (see page 147).

Lemon drizzle cake

makes: 1 x 450 g/1 lb loaf cake
health: gluten-free
cook: 45–50 minutes
store: 5 days in airtight tin. Freezes well
compost: eggshells, lemon skins

175 g/6 oz/¾ cup butter, plus extra, melted, for brushing
25 g/1 oz tapioca flour, plus extra for dusting
finely grated zest of 2 unwaxed lemons
juice of 1 lemon
2 eggs
1 tsp gluten-free baking powder
150 g/5½ oz/¾ cup granulated sugar
60 g/2¼ oz/⅔ cup ground almonds
40 g/1½ oz sorghum flour
25 g/1 oz/3 tbsp cornflour (cornstarch)
25 g/1 oz/3 tbsp polenta
1 tsp lemon oil

TOPPING

50 g/1¾ oz/¼ cup granulated sugar, plus 1 tbsp for sprinkling
juice of ½ lemon

The appeal of this cake lies in its fluffy texture and clean, uncluttered flavour. All the ingredients need to be very fresh and you must work quickly or the mixture becomes stodgy and the lemon loses its zing. It's delicious as it is, or you can warm it and serve it with crème fraîche and a dollop of homemade lemon curd – transporting you to lemon heaven.

Preheat the oven to 170°C/325°F/Gas 3. Line a 450 g/1 lb loaf tin with baking parchment, then brush with melted butter and dust with tapioca flour.

Melt the butter with the lemon zest, but don't let it get too hot. Stir well, then add the lemon juice and stir again.

Crack the eggs into a large mixing bowl. Add the baking powder, sugar, almonds, tapioca flour, sorghum flour and cornflour, polenta and lemon oil. Add the melted butter and zest mixture. Using an electric hand mixer, begin beating at low speed, then at high speed until the mixture is smooth like a batter and a rich yellow colour.

Spoon the mixture into the tin and bang it firmly on a work surface to get rid of air pockets. Bake for 30 minutes, then check and cover with baking parchment if it is getting too dark. Bake for a further 15–20 minutes, until springy to the touch. A flat cake skewer will come out clean when the cake is ready. It is quite normal for this cake to crack open along the top.

Leave the cake in its tin and, while it's still very warm, pierce all over with a skewer – don't be frightened of damaging it; you can go three-quarters of the way down into the cake. The more holes, the juicier the cake will be.

To make the topping, stir the sugar into the lemon juice and spoon over the warm cake. Use the back of the spoon to smooth the syrup over the top of the cake – this will help it seep into the holes. Leave for 10 minutes, then sprinkle the top of the cake with granulated sugar. Leave the cake to cool completely before you take it out of its tin.

For extra 'ooh-la-la'

Spread the cake generously with lemon curd once cooled.

Courgette cake

makes: 1 x 20 cm/8 in round cake
health: gluten-free
cook: 55–60 minutes
store: 1 day in airtight tin. Freezes well
compost: eggshells, courgette trimmings

2 tbsp olive oil, plus extra for brushing
50 g/1¾ oz tapioca flour, plus extra for dusting
5 eggs
225 g/8 oz/generous 1 cup light brown sugar
100 g/3½ oz sorghum flour
50 g/1¾ oz/⅓ cup cornflour (cornstarch)
2 tsp gluten-free baking powder
100 g/3½ oz/1¼ cups hazelnuts, toasted and ground
100 g/3½ oz/¾ cup macadamia nuts, toasted and roughly chopped
75 g/2¾ oz/generous ½ cup macadamia nuts, toasted and ground
grated zest of 2 limes
2 tbsp lime marmalade
½ tsp salt
225 g/8 oz/generous 1 cup grated courgettes (zucchini)

LIME DRENCH AND BUTTER ICING
100 g/3½ oz/½ cup granulated sugar
juice of 2 limes
350 g/12 oz/3 cups icing (confectioners') sugar, plus extra for dusting
grated zest and juice of 2 limes
50 g/1¾ oz/4 tbsp butter or dairy-free spread, melted

This is a delicious way to deal with a gardener's glut of courgettes. The buttery richness of the macadamias allows you to use just a dash of olive oil instead of more butter in the cake mixture.

Preheat the oven to 180°C/350°F/Gas 4. Brush 2 x 20 cm/8 in shallow cake tins with olive oil and dust with tapioca flour.

Put all of the ingredients except the courgettes into a large mixing bowl. Beat with an electric mixer until smooth, like a batter. Using a rubber spatula, stir in the grated courgettes until fully incorporated.

Divide the mixture between the prepared tins and bake for 25–30 minutes, until firm and springy to the touch. A flat cake skewer will come out clean when the cake is ready.

While the cakes are baking, prepare the lime drench. Mix the granulated sugar and lime juice, heat and stir until the sugar has dissolved.

Leave the cakes in the tins and, while still very warm, pierce all over with a skewer. You can go three-quarters of the way down into the cake. Pour the lime drench over both cakes. Put the tins on a rack to cool completely.

To make the lime butter icing, sift the icing sugar into a bowl and add the lime zest and melted butter. Beat with an electric mixer until smooth. Add the lime juice 1 teaspoon at a time – the icing must be spreadable, so you might not need to use all of the juice.

Turn out the cakes. Invert 1 of them so its flat bottom side is upwards. Spread the lime butter icing thickly over the flat surface, then sandwich the 2 halves together. Sift a little icing sugar over the top of the cake.

Make it dairy-free

Make this dairy-free as well as gluten-free by using dairy-free spread rather than butter in the icing.

Carrot cake

85 g/3 oz/6 tbsp butter, melted, plus extra for brushing
tapioca flour, for dusting
4 eggs
150 g/5½ oz/¾ cup light brown sugar
100 g/3½ oz/generous ½ cup ground brown flax seeds (linseed)
50 g/1¾ oz/generous ½ cup ground walnuts (or almonds), toasted if grinding your own
grated zest of 2 oranges
1 tsp orange oil
2 tsp mixed spice
1 tsp ground cinnamon
1½ tsp guar gum
1½ tsp gluten-free baking powder
250 g/9 oz/2¼ cups grated carrots
50 g/1¾ oz unsweetened coconut chips, roughly chopped
125 g/4½ oz/¾ cup plump raisins
50 g/1¾ oz/6 tbsp walnut pieces

ORANGE BUTTER ICING
350 g/12 oz/3 cups icing (confectioners') sugar
50 g/1¾ oz/4 tbsp butter, melted
grated zest of 2 oranges
1 tsp orange oil and 2–4 tbsp orange juice

makes: 1 x 900 g/2 lb loaf cake
health: gluten-free
cook: 45–50 minutes
store: 5 days in fridge
compost: eggshells, carrot peelings, orange skins

The high carrot content means this cake has lots of lovely antioxidant vitamins A, C and E. You don't have to ice this rustic-textured cake, but we recommend a thick layer of orange butter icing, which accentuates the zest. Dress it up further by sprinkling on fine curls of orange zest.

Preheat the oven to 170°C/325°F/Gas 3. Line a 900 g/2 lb loaf tin with baking parchment, then brush with melted butter and dust with tapioca flour.

Crack the eggs into a large mixing bowl, then add the sugar, ground flax seeds, ground walnuts, orange zest and oil, spices, guar gum and baking powder. Add the melted butter and, using an electric mixer, beat at high speed until the ingredients are well combined and the mixture is creamy.

Add the carrots, coconut, raisins and walnut pieces and stir with a rubber spatula until all the chunky ingredients are thinly coated with the creamy mixture.

Spoon the mixture into the tin and bang it firmly on a work surface to get rid of air pockets. Bake for 30 minutes, then check and cover with baking parchment if it's getting too dark or any lumpy bits are beginning to burn. Bake for a further 15–20 minutes, until firm to the touch. It develops quite a thick crust and may crack along the top. A flat cake skewer will come out clean but moist when the cake is ready. Leave the cake in its tin for 3–4 minutes and then turn out, right way up, onto a rack to cool completely. Peel off the baking parchment.

To make the orange butter icing, sift the icing sugar into a bowl, then add the melted butter, orange zest and orange oil and beat with an electric mixer. Add the orange juice gradually, until the icing is of a spreadable consistency (you may not need to use all the juice). Spread the icing thickly over the top of the cake.

Give it a twist

For added moistness, pre-soak the raisins in orange juice, then heat gently until they have plumped out. Drain off the orange juice before adding the raisins to the cake mixture. This orange juice can then be used to make the icing.

Coffee, whiskey and hazelnut cake

500 g/1 lb 2 oz/2¼ cups butter, melted, plus extra for brushing
100 g/3½ oz tapioca flour, plus extra for dusting
8 eggs
450 g/1 lb/2¼ cups light brown sugar
200 g/7 oz sorghum flour
100 g/3½ oz/1 cup cornflour (cornstarch)
4 tsp gluten-free baking powder
200 g/7 oz/1½ cups hazelnuts, toasted and chopped
150 g/5½ oz/generous 1 cup hazelnuts, toasted and ground
2 tbsp espresso coffee granules
chocolate-covered coffee beans, to decorate

COFFEE DRENCH

1½ tbsp espresso coffee granules
1½ tbsp granulated sugar
1½ tbsp Irish whiskey
150 ml/5 fl oz/⅔ cup boiling water

COFFEE LIQUEUR ICING

900 g/2 lb/7½ cups icing (confectioners') sugar
5 tbsp Irish cream liqueur
300 g/10½ oz/1¼ cups butter, melted
2 tsp vanilla extract
1–2 tbsp whole milk (if required)

makes: 1 x deep 20 cm/8 in round cake
health: gluten-free
cook: 30–35 minutes
store: 2 days in airtight tin
compost: eggshells

This is a grown-up party piece. It is a massive beast of a cake – you will need a very large mixing bowl and/or a large food processor.

Preheat the oven to 180°C/350°F/Gas 4. Brush 3 x 20 cm/8 in shallow cake tins with melted butter and dust with tapioca flour.

Put all of the cake ingredients and 1 tsp salt into a large mixing bowl and beat with an electric mixer at high speed for 2–3 minutes, until thick and creamy. Scrape down the sides of the bowl with a rubber spatula. Divide the mixture between the 3 tins and bake for 30–35 minutes, until firm and springy to the touch.

Meanwhile, prepare the coffee drench. Mix the coffee, sugar and whiskey in a jug, add the boiling water and stir until the sugar dissolves.

You need to slice the rounded top off 1 of the cakes – a quarter to a fifth of its depth. Keep this slice of cake to use for the crumb decoration.

While the 3 cakes are still warm, pierce them all over with a skewer. Pour roughly equal amounts of the hot coffee drench over each of the cakes. Leave in the tins to cool. Turn out onto a rack covered in baking parchment. You will now be looking at their flat bottoms. Blitz the reserved slice of cake in a food processor to a breadcrumb-like consistency.

To make the coffee liqueur icing, sift the icing sugar into a bowl and add the liqueur, melted butter and vanilla. Beat with an electric mixer until smooth and spreadable. It mustn't be sloppy, but it should be easy to apply. If necessary, add milk or more liqueur, a tablespoon or so at a time, to loosen the icing.

Spread each sponge with the icing, and then layer them up with the thinner cake (from which you removed a slice) in the middle. Spread icing over the sides and top of the cake. Spread the cake crumbs on a clean surface and roll your cake in the crumbs. Decorate with chocolate-coated coffee beans.

For a smaller cake

Make half quantities for a 23 cm/9 in springform tin or 900 g/2 lb loaf tin. The baking time stays the same. Slice in half and sandwich with icing.

Sticky date cake

makes: 1 x 900 g/2 lb loaf cake
health: gluten-free
cook: 35–40 minutes
store: 10 days in airtight tin. Freezes well
compost: eggshells

melted butter, for brushing
tapioca flour, for dusting
250 g/9 oz pitted dates, chopped
1 tsp baking soda
¼ tsp cream of tartar
2 eggs
75 g/2¾ oz/¾ cup ground almonds
70 g/2½ oz sorghum flour
2 tbsp almond oil
3 tbsp maple syrup

BUTTERSCOTCH TOPPING

60 g/2¼ oz/4½ tbsp butter
5 tbsp muscovado sugar
2 tbsp double (heavy) cream

The texture of this loaf is quite fudge-like – it's got a high fruit content. The topping is simple to make and sets quite solidly – so you can easily transport slices in packed lunch boxes.

Preheat the oven to 180°C/350°F/Gas 4. Line a 900 g/2 lb loaf tin with baking parchment, then brush with melted butter and dust with tapioca flour.

Put the dates and 100 ml/3½ fl oz water into a pan and bring to the boil. Add the baking soda and cream of tartar and stir for a couple of seconds with a wooden spoon until the dates have soaked up the water and the baking soda and cream of tartar have dissolved. Remove the pan from the heat.

Crack the eggs into a large mixing bowl and add the almonds, sorghum flour, almond oil and maple syrup. Using an electric mixer, begin beating at low speed, then at high speed until the ingredients are just combined. Add the date mixture and stir with a rubber spatula; you need to scrape right to the bottom of the bowl – don't worry, you can't overmix this cake. It almost looks curdled at this stage, but keep calm and carry on.

Spoon into the tin and bang the tin firmly on a work surface to get rid of air pockets. Bake for 25 minutes, then check and cover with baking parchment if any lumps are beginning to burn. Bake for a further 10–15 minutes, until a flat cake skewer comes out clean. Please note this isn't the prettiest of cakes. While baking it develops a thick, dark 'rhino skin' and it is normal for the surface to crack. Leave the cake in its tin for 10 minutes while you make the topping.

To make the butterscotch topping, put all the ingredients into a pan and heat until the sugar has dissolved and the mixture is beginning to bubble. Remove from the heat and beat well until smooth. Turn the cake out of its tin, the right way up, onto a rack. Stir the sauce well and pour over the still-warm cake. Leave to cool.

For extra 'ooh-la-la'

For extra crunch, scatter the topping with crushed praline (see page 41).

Coconut and lime cake

almond oil and tapioca flour, for brushing
200 ml/7 fl oz/scant 1 cup canned coconut milk
250 g/9 oz unsweetened coconut chips, chopped
100 g/3½ oz/½ cup caster (superfine) sugar
1 tsp gluten-free baking powder
1 tsp salt
100 g/3½ oz/1 cup ground almonds
85 g/3 oz sorghum flour
juice of 1 lime
2 tbsp lime cordial
8 egg whites

LIME DRENCH

3 tbsp lime cordial
3 tbsp granulated sugar

LIME BUTTER ICING

350 g/12 oz/3 cups icing (confectioners') sugar
juice and grated zest of 2–3 limes
50 g/1¾ oz/4 tbsp butter or dairy-free spread, melted

makes: 1 x 20 cm/8 in round cake
health: gluten-free (dairy-free if dairy-free spread used)
cook: 25 minutes
store: 3 days in airtight tin. Freezes well
compost: eggshells, lime skins

You can use grated fresh coconut instead of dried coconut chips; if you have a fresh coconut you can also use some of the drained coconut water instead of the canned coconut milk. For an impressive finish you can scatter the top of the cake with finely shaved curls of lime zest (remove zest from the lime before you squeeze it for the cake mixture).

Preheat the oven to 180°C/350°F/Gas 4. Line 2 x 20 cm/8 in shallow cake tins with discs of baking parchment, then brush with almond oil and dust with tapioca flour.

If the coconut milk has separated and a crust has formed, blitz it in a food processor. Put the chopped coconut chips into a large mixing bowl. Add the coconut milk, sugar, baking powder, salt, almonds, sorghum flour, lime juice and lime cordial. Beat with an electric mixer until well combined.

In a separate large bowl, whisk the egg whites until they form stiff peaks. Using a rubber spatula, fold the whites into the coconut mixture. They need to be fully incorporated, but try not to overmix. Divide the mixture between the tins. Bake for 25 minutes, until well risen, golden brown and firm to the touch. They may crack along the top. A flat cake skewer will come out clean when they are ready.

While the cakes are baking, prepare the lime drench: mix the lime, sugar and 1 tbsp water and heat, stirring well, until the sugar has dissolved. Leave the cakes in the tins and, while still very warm, pierce all over with a skewer. Pour the lime drench over them. Put the tins on a rack to cool.

To make the lime butter icing, sift the icing sugar into a bowl and add the lime zest and juice. Then add the melted butter and beat with an electric mixer until smooth and spreadable. If it is too stiff, you may need to add more lime juice; if it is too runny, add more icing sugar.

Turn out the cakes and peel off the baking parchment. Invert one of them so its flat bottom side is upwards. Spread the icing thickly over the flat surface, then sandwich the 2 cakes together.

Make it dairy-free

Make this dairy-free as well as gluten-free by using dairy-free spread rather than butter in the icing.

Ginger hippo cake

makes: 20 cm/8 in round cake
health: gluten-free
cook: 25–30 minutes
store: 5 days in fridge. Freezes well
compost: eggshells

This whimsical cake delights everyone. Even those who claim not to like ginger or anything gluten-free are won over by it.

- 175 g/6 oz/¾ cup butter, melted, plus extra for brushing
- tapioca flour, for dusting
- 100 g/3½ oz stem ginger in syrup (drained weight)
- 4 eggs
- 175 g/6 oz/generous ¾ cup light brown sugar
- 125 g/4½ oz/1¼ cups ground almonds
- 100 g/3½ oz sorghum flour
- 2 tsp ground ginger
- 1 tsp gluten-free baking powder
- icing (confectioner's) sugar, for dusting

MASCARPONE FILLING

- 250 g/9 oz mascarpone
- 50 g/1¾ oz stem ginger in syrup (drained weight)
- 5–6 tbsp ginger jam (optional)

Preheat the oven to 180°C/350°F/Gas 4. Brush 2 x 20 cm/8 in shallow cake tins with melted butter and dust with tapioca flour.

Crush the stem ginger, using a food processor or blender and put it into a mixing bowl. Add the eggs, sugar, almonds, sorghum flour, ground ginger, baking powder and melted butter and beat with an electric mixer until creamy.

Divide the mixture between the tins. Bake for 25–30 minutes, until risen and springy to the touch. A flat cake skewer will come out clean when the cake is ready. Turn the cakes out onto a rack and leave to cool completely.

For the filling, whizz up the mascarpone and stem ginger in a food processor.

When the cakes are cold, spread the ginger jam, if using, thickly over the flat bottom of 1 of the sponges, then spread the gingery mascarpone over the jam and sandwich the 2 cakes together.

Draw your hippos on a piece of card and cut out. Put the hippos around the edge of the cake and sift icing sugar over the top. With a steady hand, carefully lift off your hippo shapes and you'll have a unique ginger hippo cake.

Hippo template

For extra 'ooh-la-la'

You can use stem ginger syrup as a drench: when you take the cakes out of the oven, pierce them all over and pour the syrup over. If you want a richer cake, use muscovado sugar in place of light brown sugar. Adding 1 tsp ground allspice would give more depth of flavour.

St Martha's chocolate and orange cake

325 g/11½ oz/1¼ cups butter, melted, plus extra for brushing
tapioca flour, for dusting
4 oranges
1½ tsp orange oil
4 eggs
300 g/10½ oz/1½ cups granulated sugar
1 tsp gluten-free baking powder
200 g/7 oz/2 cups ground almonds
115 g/4 oz/scant 1 cup polenta
60 g/2¼ oz/¾ cup hazelnuts, ground
200 g/7 oz dark chocolate, chopped

ORANGE DRENCH

3 tbsp granulated sugar

CHOCOLATE DRIZZLE

50 g/1¾ oz dark chocolate, chopped
1 tsp olive oil

makes: 1 x 23 cm/9 in round cake
health: gluten-free
cook: 40–45 minutes
store: 7 days in airtight tin. Freezes well
compost: eggshells, orange skins

It's inevitable that some of the chocolate chunks will sink to the bottom, but when a cake tastes this good that'll be the last thing on your mind!

Preheat the oven to 180°C/350°F/Gas 4. Line a 23 cm/9 in round springform tin with a disc of baking parchment, then brush with melted butter and dust with tapioca flour.

Grate the zest from all 4 oranges and squeeze the juice from 3. Mix the melted butter with the orange zest, a third of the juice and the orange oil.

Crack the eggs into a large mixing bowl, then add the sugar, baking powder, almonds, polenta and hazelnuts. Add the melted butter mixture and beat with an electric mixer at high speed until light and smooth. Stir in the chocolate chunks using a rubber spatula.

Spoon the mixture into the tin. Bake for 20 minutes. Cover the cake with a piece of baking parchment to prevent it from burning and bake for a further 20–25 minutes, until risen and springy to the touch. A flat cake skewer will come out clean when the cake is ready. This cake may crack across the top.

Meanwhile, prepare the orange drench: mix the remaining orange juice with the sugar and heat, stirring well, until the sugar is just starting to dissolve.

Leave the cake in the tin and, while still warm, pierce all over with a skewer. Pour the orange drench over the top. Put the tin on a rack to cool. Turn out and place on a plate, the right way up, and peel off the baking parchment. To decorate, melt the dark chocolate with the olive oil in a heatproof bowl set over a saucepan of gently simmering water, stirring until smooth (or in a microwave). Drizzle the chocolate off a metal spoon into a squiggly pattern on top of the cake. Leave to set.

For extra 'ooh-la-la'

Replace the orange juice with Grand Marnier in the drench.

Caramel, pecan and dark chocolate cake

makes: 1 x 900 g/2 lb loaf cake
health: gluten-free
cook: 35–40 minutes
store: 3 days in airtight tin. Freezes well
compost: eggshells, sweet wrappers if compostable

melted butter, for brushing
tapioca flour, for dusting
8 egg whites
100 g/3½ oz gluten-free chewy caramels, chopped into quarters
150 g/5½ oz dark chocolate, chopped
100 g/3½ oz/1 cup pecans, toasted and ground
100 g/3½ oz/1 cup ground almonds
75 g/2¾ oz/⅓ cup muscovado sugar
75 g/2¾ oz sorghum flour
50 g/1¾ oz dulce de leche
1½ tsp gluten-free baking powder
½ tsp salt

CARAMELIZED PECANS

100 g/3½ oz/1 cup pecan halves
1 tbsp muscovado sugar
½ tbsp butter
1 tsp salt

PRALINE

25 g/1 oz/¼ cup pecans, toasted
60 g/2¼ oz/5 tbsp caster (superfine) sugar

STICKY TOPPING

60 g/2¼ oz dulce de leche
2 tbsp clotted or double (heavy) cream

This cake looks really lovely with its glittery jacket of crushed praline. If you're in a rush, you can skip the praline; alternatively, you can prepare it ahead of time – as well as the caramelized pecans and toasted ground pecans. I love this combination of sweet caramel with the slightly salted pecans, but you can reduce the salt if you wish. Look for a gluten-free brand of caramels or soft toffees.

Preheat the oven to 180°C/350°F/Gas 4. Brush a 900 g/2 lb loaf tin with melted butter and dust with tapioca flour.

To make the caramelized pecans, put the pecans into a wide, heavy-bottomed pan with the sugar, butter and salt. Stir continuously over a high heat until the sugar has dissolved. This takes about 5–6 minutes. Leave to cool slightly. Put the pecans in a food processor and pulse a couple of times to chop roughly.

In a large mixing bowl, whisk the egg whites until they form stiff peaks. Add the caramelized pecans and remaining cake ingredients. Using a rubber spatula, fold together until all the ingredients are evenly blended. Spoon into the tin. Bake for 30–35 minutes, until firm and slightly springy to the touch. Leave in its tin for a couple of minutes, then turn out onto a rack.

To make the praline, spread the toasted pecans on a baking sheet covered with baking parchment. Sprinkle with a pinch of salt. Put the sugar in a pan over a low heat until the sugar dissolves and turns golden; stir with a wooden spoon. Carefully remove from the heat and pour over the nuts. Leave to set and cool – about 5 minutes. Break up the praline into chunks and blitz in the food processor.

For the sticky topping, put the ingredients into a small pan and heat until just starting to bubble. Stir, then spoon over the cooled cake. Sprinkle the praline over the cake. Leave the cake to cool before you take it out of its tin.

Make the most of your freezer

You can make caramelized pecans and plain toasted pecans in advance and freeze them. Make double the amount of praline: it keeps for ages in a screw-topped jar and can be used as a topping for baked apples and other puds. It may stick together, but just blitz in a food processor.

Chocolate, hazelnut and cranberry cake

makes: 1 x 20 cm/8 in round cake
health: gluten-free
cook: 25–28 minutes
store: sponge 10 days in airtight tin. Freezes well
compost: eggshells

125 g/4½ oz/generous ½ cup butter, melted, plus extra for brushing
tapioca flour, for dusting
2 eggs
185 g/6½ oz/scant 2 cups ground almonds
185 g/6½ oz/scant 2 cups hazelnuts, ground
1 tsp gluten-free baking powder
1 tsp guar gum
150 g/5½ oz/¾ cup light brown sugar
100 g/3½ oz/1 cup dried cranberries
50 g/1¾ oz/scant ½ cup polenta
1 tsp vanilla extract
175 ml/6 fl oz/¾ cup whole milk
2 tbsp brandy or hazelnut syrup
100 g/3½ oz dark chocolate, chopped
1–2 tbsp cocoa powder, for dusting

HAZELNUT BUTTER

25 g/1 oz/¼ cup hazelnuts, toasted
100 g/3½ oz/scant ½ cup butter, melted
50 g/1¾ oz/⅔ cup hazelnuts, ground
50 g/1¾ oz/¼ cup light brown sugar

CHOCOLATE GANACHE

250 ml/9 fl oz/generous 1 cup double (heavy) cream
225 g/8 oz dark chocolate, chopped

We call this 'Coppice cake' in honour of the craft that helps to maintain our ancient woodlands. Enjoy this as an everyday cake, or add hazelnut butter and chocolate ganache for a special occasion – and decorate with roses, rose hips or hedgerow berries.

Preheat the oven to 180°C/350°F/Gas 4. Line 2 x 20 cm/8 in round shallow cake tins with parchment, then brush with melted butter and dust with tapioca flour.

Crack the eggs into a mixing bowl, then add the ground almonds and hazelnuts, baking powder, guar gum, sugar, cranberries, polenta and vanilla. Put the melted butter, milk and brandy into a separate bowl, stir briefly and then pour into the first mixing bowl. Mix with an electric mixer until the mixture lightens in colour and becomes thick and creamy. Stir in the chocolate chunks using a rubber spatula.

Divide the mixture between the tins and flatten with a spatula. Bake for 20 minutes, then check and cover with baking parchment if browning too quickly. Bake for a further 5–8 minutes, until firm and springy to the touch. Leave in the tins to cool to room temperature, then transfer to the fridge for 2 hours.

To make the hazelnut butter, chop the toasted hazelnuts, then mix all the ingredients together in a bowl using a wooden spoon. Chill until needed. You may need to soften it slightly to make it spreadable.

Turn out the cakes and peel off the parchment. Place 1 on a serving plate, flat side up. Spoon the hazelnut butter onto the cake and spread it using a palette knife. Lay the other cake on top.

To make the ganache, heat the cream in a heavy-bottomed pan until it starts to bubble. Remove from the heat and stir in the chocolate. Beat until the chocolate has melted. Spoon over the cake, spreading with a palette knife. Chill for about 30 minutes. Finish with a dusting of cocoa powder and decorate with fresh roses.

For extra 'ooh-la-la'

To use fresh roses for decoration, first shake off any wildlife. Cut the stems about 3 cm/1 in below the flower. Wrap a small piece of damp cotton wool around the end of the stem, then wrap in a small piece of foil. Keep in the fridge until needed. Push gently into the cake.

Holwell Village Hall scones

makes: 6 fat scones
health: gluten-free
cook: 10 minutes
store: 3 days in airtight tin. Freeze well
compost: eggshells

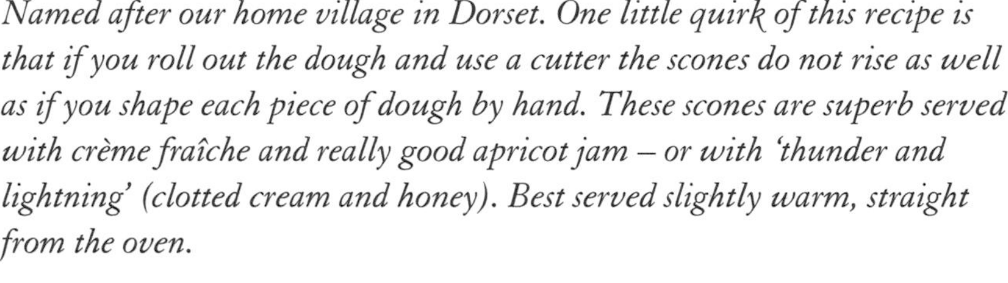

Named after our home village in Dorset. One little quirk of this recipe is that if you roll out the dough and use a cutter the scones do not rise as well as if you shape each piece of dough by hand. These scones are superb served with crème fraîche and really good apricot jam – or with 'thunder and lightning' (clotted cream and honey). Best served slightly warm, straight from the oven.

200 g/7 oz/1¼ cups ground almonds
2 eggs
50 g/1¾ oz/¼ cup light brown sugar
85 g/3 oz sorghum flour, plus extra for dusting
2 tsp gluten-free baking powder
½ tsp guar gum
pinch of salt
2 tbsp almond oil
2 tsp vanilla extract
whole milk, for brushing
brown vanilla sugar, for sprinkling

Preheat the oven to 180°C/350°F/Gas 4. Line a baking tray with a piece of baking parchment.

Put the almonds, eggs, sugar, sorghum flour, baking powder, guar gum, salt, almond oil and vanilla into a food processor and blitz until fully incorporated. The resulting dough should be slightly sticky. If it is too sticky, add up to 3 tbsp extra sorghum flour, 1 tbsp at a time. If too dry, add a little more almond oil.

Dust your hands and the work surface with sorghum flour. Knead the dough briefly and then divide it into 6 roughly equal portions. Lightly roll them into balls and then slightly flatten them so they're 3–5 cm/1¼–2 in thick.

Place the scones, evenly spaced, on the baking sheet. Brush them with milk and sprinkle with brown vanilla sugar. Bake for 10 minutes or until golden on top.

For extra 'ooh-la-la'

Add 100 g/3½ oz chopped soft dried apricots to the scone mixture.

FOR HOME &
HOLWEL

muffins

Strawberry and cream muffins

makes: 10–12 muffins
health: gluten-free
cook: 18–20 minutes
store: best eaten on same day. Freeze well (without cream and topping)
compost: eggshells, strawberry trimmings

- 100 g/3½ oz/scant ½ cup butter, melted, plus extra for brushing
- 100 g/3½ oz/½ cup granulated sugar
- 85 g/3 oz/scant ¾ cup polenta
- 75 g/2¾ oz/¾ cup ground almonds
- 50 g/1¾ oz sorghum flour
- 1½ tsp guar gum
- 1½ tsp gluten-free baking powder
- 2 eggs
- 100 g/3½ oz clotted cream or crème fraîche
- 3 tbsp whole milk
- 1 tsp vanilla extract
- 200 g/7 oz/1¼ cups strawberries, hulled and sliced
- freshly ground black pepper

TOPPING

- 100 g/3½ oz clotted cream, or double (heavy) cream, whipped until thick
- 5–6 strawberries, halved
- icing (confectioners') sugar, for dusting (optional)

I love the rich creaminess of these muffins. They are heavenly when served warm from the oven: have a bowl of clotted cream at the ready, and be prepared for it to melt onto your warm muffins… messily and deliciously. Alternatively, if you allow them to cool completely, you can decorate them with a dollop of cream and a strawberry, or present as butterfly cake (see below).

Preheat the oven to 180°C/350°F/Gas 4. Brush a 12-cup silicone muffin pan with melted butter and place on a metal baking sheet.

Put the sugar, polenta, almonds, sorghum flour, guar gum and baking powder into a bowl and mix with a fork.

Put the melted butter into a large mixing bowl, then add the eggs, cream, milk and vanilla and beat with an electric mixer at high speed.

Add the dry ingredients to the wet and, using a rubber spatula, mix in quickly – just until all the ingredients are combined. Add the sliced strawberries and mix gently to combine. Scrape down the sides of the bowl to ensure everything is mixed in, but take care not to mush up the strawberries by being over-vigorous.

Spoon the mixture into the muffin cups. Pile them high for 10 big muffins or make 12 smaller ones. Grind a little black pepper over each muffin. Bake for 18–20 minutes, until gently domed and springy to the touch. Eat warm or turn them out onto a rack and leave to cool completely.

To make butterfly cakes, cut a 2–3 cm/1 in diameter slice across the dome of each muffin, then cut each slice in half and set aside. Top each muffin with 1 tsp cream, then gently push both halves of the muffin slice into the cream at jaunty angles. Place a halved strawberry on top. If you like, dust with icing sugar.

For extra 'ooh-la-la'

These muffins work really well baked in heart-shaped silicone moulds. You can also pre-soak the fresh strawberries for the topping in sparkling wine.

Upside-down peach muffins

makes: 12 muffins
health: gluten-free, dairy-free
cook: 38–40 minutes
store: best eaten on same day; 2 days in airtight container in fridge. Freeze well
compost: eggshells, peach stones

4 tbsp almond oil, plus extra for brushing
100 g/3½ oz/¾ cup almonds, toasted and chopped
75 g/2¾ oz/¾ cup ground almonds
75 g/2¾ oz/scant ⅔ cup polenta
50 g/1¾ oz tapioca flour
1½ tsp gluten-free baking powder
1½ tsp guar gum
2 eggs
100 ml/3½ fl oz/7 tbsp clear honey
4 tbsp amaretto

ROASTED PEACH PURÉE

2 large peaches, pitted and sliced into eighths
5 tbsp clear honey
juice of 1 lemon

TOPPING

2 peaches
2–3 tbsp praline (see page 41), crushed

These peachy-bottomed delights make lovely individual puddings. They're best served warm with crème fraîche or mascarpone, and drizzled with honey. Alternatively, mix the reserved peach juice with mascarpone and amaretto and spoon over the muffins whilst warm for a grown-up accompaniment.

Preheat the oven to 180°C/350°F/Gas 4. Brush a 12-cup bendy silicone muffin pan with almond oil and place on a metal baking sheet.

To make the roasted peach purée, put the peaches into a roasting pan. Drizzle the honey and lemon juice over them. Bake for 20 minutes. Drain off any juice and set aside (see introduction), then purée the peaches in a food processor. Weigh out 200 g/7 oz for the muffin mixture; save any remaining for another day.

Put the chopped almonds, ground almonds, polenta, tapioca flour, baking powder and guar gum into a bowl and mix with a fork.

Crack the eggs into a large mixing bowl. Add the 200 g/7 oz peach purée, together with the honey, almond oil and amaretto and beat with an electric mixer at high speed until slightly frothy.

Add the dry ingredients to the wet and, using a rubber spatula, mix in quickly – just until all the ingredients are combined. Scrape down the sides of the bowl to ensure everything is mixed in, but don't overmix.

For the topping, cut each peach in half, remove the stone, then cut each half into 3 or 4 slices. Cover the bottom of each muffin cup with peach slices – this should leave about two-thirds of the cup for the muffin mixture.

Spoon the muffin mixture into the muffin cups. Bake for 18–20 minutes, until gently domed and springy to the touch.

Place a piece of baking parchment over a rack and turn out the muffins, upside down. Sprinkle crushed praline over the bottoms. You may need to realign the peach slices with a palette knife and push them back into the muffins.

Give it a twist

Use nectarines or plums instead of peaches.

Baked apple muffins

125 g/4½ oz/¾ cup light brown sugar
100 g/3½ oz/⅔ cup raisins
75 g/2¾ oz/scant ⅔ cup polenta
75 g/2¾ oz/¾ cup ground almonds
50 g/1¾ oz gluten-free oat flour
2 tsp ground cinnamon
1½ tsp mixed spice
1½ tsp guar gum
1½ tsp gluten-free baking powder
1 tsp baking soda
pinch of salt
2 eggs
100 g/3½ oz/7 tbsp Greek yogurt
4 tbsp whole milk
3 tbsp almond oil

BAKED APPLE PURÉE

500 g/1 lb 2 oz cooking apples
5 tbsp clear honey
juice of 1 lemon
2 tsp ground cinnamon

TOPPING

2–3 tsp cinnamon sugar
2–3 tbsp praline (see page 41), crushed

makes: 12 muffins
health: gluten-free
cook: 38–40 minutes
store: best eaten on same day; 2 days in airtight container in fridge. Freeze
compost: eggshells, apple trimmings

Like the Dorset apple cake (page 26), this recipe is ideal for using up spare fruits. We use any variety of apple we have to hand and we've not been disappointed yet. Baking the apples before adding them to the muffin mixture maximises the flavour of the fruit; it's worth that little extra effort.

Preheat the oven to 180°C/350°F/Gas 4. Line a 12-cup muffin pan with paper muffin cases.

To make the baked apple purée, peel and core the apples, then cut them into eighths. Put them in a baking dish, add the honey, lemon juice and cinnamon and mix. Bake for 20 minutes. After baking, pop the apples and juices into a food processor and whizz to a purée. Weigh out 250 g/9 oz for the muffin mixture and set aside the remainder for the topping.

Put the sugar, raisins, polenta, almonds, oat flour, cinnamon, mixed spice, guar gum, baking powder, baking soda and salt into a bowl and mix with a fork.

Crack the eggs into a large mixing bowl. Add the 250 g/9 oz reserved baked apple purée, together with the yogurt, milk and almond oil and beat with an electric mixer at high speed until combined.

Add the dry ingredients to the wet and, using a rubber spatula, mix in quickly – just until all the ingredients are combined. Scrape down the sides of the bowl to ensure everything is mixed in, but don't overmix.

Spoon the muffin mixture into the paper cases. Top each muffin with ½ tsp apple purée and dredge with cinnamon sugar. Bake for 18–20 minutes, until gently domed and springy to the touch.

Lift the muffins onto a rack: if left in the pan they will go soggy. Sprinkle some praline over each muffin while they are still warm.

Love your leftovers

Freeze any leftover apple purée. Serve it mixed with a dash of Calvados to accompany these muffins served as a pudding, or with your Dorset apple cake.

Raspberry and very chocolatey muffins

makes: 24 mini muffins
health: gluten-free
cook: 15 minutes
store: best eaten on same day; 2 days in fridge. Freeze well
compost: eggshells

- 75 g/2¾ oz/5 tbsp butter, plus extra, melted, for brushing
- 200 g/7 oz dark chocolate, chopped
- 75 g/2¾ oz/⅓ cup light brown sugar
- 70 g/2½ oz/scant 1 cup hazelnuts, ground
- 60 g/2¼ oz/½ cup polenta
- 40 g/1½ oz sorghum flour
- 10 g/¼ oz freeze-dried raspberries, crumbled
- 1½ tbsp cocoa powder
- 1 tsp gluten-free baking powder
- 1 tsp guar gum
- pinch of salt
- 1 egg
- 85 g/3 oz/⅓ cup Greek yogurt
- 5 tbsp orange or raspberry juice

DRUNKEN RASPBERRIES

- 24 fresh raspberries
- 3–4 tbsp raspberry liqueur or amaretto

TOPPING

- 125 g/4½ oz dark chocolate, chopped
- 1 tbsp almond oil
- 8–24 raspberries
- 1 tbsp freeze-dried raspberries, crumbled
- 6 fresh rose buds (optional)

This magnificently chocolatey mixture is very rich. You can have fun with mixing and matching the toppings. One weekend we decorated lots of them with molten, glossy dark chocolate and a mixture of crumbled freeze-dried raspberries, whole chocolate-dipped fresh raspberries and tiny rose buds.

To make the drunken raspberries, soak the raspberries in the liqueur for at least an hour, or overnight. Preheat the oven to 180°C/350°F/Gas 4. Brush a 24-cup bendy silicone mini muffin pan with melted butter and place on a metal baking sheet.

Melt the butter with 125 g/4½ oz of the chocolate in a heatproof bowl set over a saucepan of gently simmering water, stirring until smooth (or in a microwave). Allow the mixture to cool slightly.

Put the remaining 75 g/2¾ oz chocolate into a bowl. Add the sugar, hazelnuts, polenta, sorghum flour, crumbled raspberries, cocoa powder, baking powder, guar gum and salt and mix with a fork.

Put the egg, yogurt and orange juice into a large mixing bowl. Add the melted butter mixture and beat with an electric mixer at high speed. Add the dry ingredients to the wet and, using a rubber spatula, mix in quickly – just until all the ingredients are combined. Scrape down the sides of the bowl to ensure everything is mixed in, but don't overmix.

Spoon the mixture into the muffin cups, half-filling them. Pop a drunken raspberry on top of this mixture, 1 in each cup. Spoon in the remaining mixture to fill each cup. Bake for 15 minutes, until gently domed and springy to the touch. Leave for 2–3 minutes, then turn out onto a rack.

To make the topping, melt the chocolate with the almond oil in a heatproof bowl set over a saucepan of gently simmering water, stirring until smooth. Dip the top of each muffin into the chocolate. Add a raspberry (half-dipped in the melted chocolate if you like) to the top of each muffin. You could sprinkle crumbled freeze-dried raspberries on some muffins and pop a fresh rose bud on others.

Great for kids

For a non-alcoholic version, use raspberry jam (¼ tsp per muffin) instead of drunken raspberries.

Get-out-of-bed banana muffins

makes: 12–14 muffins
health: gluten-free, dairy-free
cook: 20 minutes
store: best eaten on same day; 2 days in airtight container in fridge. Freeze well
compost: eggshells, banana skins

- vegetable oil, for brushing
- 55 g/2 oz dried banana chips
- 185 g/6½ oz gluten-free oat flour or ground brown flax seeds (linseed)
- 50 g/1¾ oz gluten-free oats or millet flakes
- 100 g/3½ oz/generous ½ cup plump raisins
- 70 g/2½ oz/½ cup almonds, toasted and chopped
- 25 g/1 oz/¼ cup ground almonds
- 1½ tsp ground cinnamon
- 1½ tsp guar gum
- 1½ tsp gluten-free baking powder
- 2 egg whites
- 200 ml/7 fl oz/scant 1 cup soya milk
- 100 ml/3½ fl oz/7 tbsp clear honey
- 2 large bananas

TOPPING

- 2 bananas
- 2–3 tbsp cinnamon sugar

What better reason do you need to spring out of bed in the morning than these little beauties? They're a healthy quick breakfast option that doesn't feel too 'goody two shoes'. They're very low in fat and refined sugar, dairy-free and, of course, gluten-free. If you use ground brown flax seeds (linseed) instead of the gluten-free oats, you'll be getting the heart-healthy and brain-boosting powers of omega-3 fats as well. The only fiddly bit is grinding the banana chips to make 'banana flour': this doesn't work with semi-dried banana pieces – it just gets too sticky.

Preheat the oven to 180°C/350°F/Gas 4. Brush 14 x mini-loaf tins (7 x 4 cm/2¾ x 1½ in) with vegetable oil and place on a baking sheet. (Alternatively, use a 12-cup silicone muffin pan, lightly brushed with vegetable oil, then placed on a metal baking sheet.)

In a food processor, whizz the dried banana chips to a fine powder, then put them into a bowl. Add the oat flour, oats, raisins, chopped and ground almonds, cinnamon, guar gum and baking powder and mix with a fork.

Put the egg whites, soya milk and honey into a large mixing bowl and beat with an electric mixer at high speed until slightly frothy. Break the bananas into small chunks, about 2 cm/¾ in, and stir into the mixture using a rubber spatula.

Add the dry ingredients to the wet and, using a rubber spatula, mix in quickly – just until all the ingredients are combined. Scrape down the sides of the bowl to ensure everything is mixed in, but don't overmix.

Spoon the mixture into the loaf tins or muffin cups, filling to nearly the top. For the topping, slice the bananas and put 3 slices on each loaf or muffin, then sprinkle with cinnamon sugar.

Bake for 20 minutes, until golden, gently domed and springy to the touch. Leave for 2–3 minutes, then carefully turn out on to a rack.

For your lunch box

These little loaves are perfect portable snacks. Eaten at lunchtime, their slow-release energy will help to prevent the afternoon slumps.

Marvellous marmalade muffins

1 orange
125 g/4½ oz/generous ½ cup light brown sugar
100 g/3½ oz/generous ½ cup plump raisins
85 g/3 oz/scant ¾ cup polenta
75 g/2¾ oz/¾ cup ground almonds
50 g/1¾ oz/scant ½ cup pistachios, toasted and chopped
50 g/1¾ oz quinoa flour
1½ tsp guar gum
1½ tsp gluten-free baking powder
1 tsp baking soda
100 g/3½ oz/scant ½ cup butter, melted
2 eggs
100 ml/3½ fl oz orange juice

FILLING AND TOPPING

2 tbsp orange marmalade
2 tbsp pistachios, toasted and chopped

makes: 12 muffins
health: gluten-free
cook: 18–20 minutes
store: best eaten on same day; 2–3 days in airtight container. Freeze well
compost: eggshells

The quality of the marmalade really does shine through in these muffins – it's not worth economizing here. We use a brilliant tangerine and lemon marmalade made by our friend Susan, who is the reigning national 'Jampion' of the UK Jam & Chutney Makers.

Preheat the oven to 180°C/350°F/Gas 4. Line a 12-cup muffin pan with paper muffin cases.

Cut the orange into quarters, then halve these. Pop everything (including zest and pips) into a food processor and blitz to a pulp. Set aside.

Put the sugar, raisins, polenta, almonds, pistachios, quinoa flour, guar gum, baking powder and baking soda into a bowl and mix with a fork.

Put the melted butter, eggs and orange juice into a large mixing bowl and beat with an electric mixer at high speed until slightly frothy. Add the pulped orange and stir it in using a rubber spatula.

Add the dry ingredients to the wet and, using a rubber spatula, mix in quickly – just until all the ingredients are combined. Scrape down the sides of the bowl to ensure everything is mixed in, but don't overmix and don't worry if there are still a few little blobs of dry mixture visible.

Spoon some of the muffin mixture into the paper cases to about half-full. Add ½ tsp marmalade to each muffin, then fill up the paper cases with more muffin mixture and sprinkle a few chopped pistachios over each one.

Bake for 18–20 minutes, until light to mid-brown, gently domed and springy to the touch. Leave for 2–3 minutes, then carefully turn them out on to a rack.

Hazelnut cappuccino cupcakes

makes: 12 cupcakes
health: gluten-free
cook: 18–20 minutes
store: best eaten on same day; 2–3 days in airtight container. Freeze well
compost: eggshells

These sophisticated little cakes don't rise much, so they have quite flat tops, which are all the better for icing. You're aiming for a cappuccino-like finish, with a dusting of cocoa powder or cinnamon. They are gorgeous as an accompaniment to a mid-morning espresso. Alternatively, include them in a spread of other delicate party pieces, such as Iced gems (page 140) or Bourbon creams (page 126). Invite some girlfriends over, let them know it's a posh frock do and serve on Gran's fine bone china.

- 100 g/3½ oz/¾ cup hazelnuts, toasted and ground
- 125 g/4½ oz/generous ½ cup caster (superfine) sugar
- 25 g/1 oz tapioca flour
- 1 tbsp good instant espresso granules
- 1 tsp gluten-free baking powder
- 2 eggs
- 2 tbsp whole milk
- 1 tbsp hazelnut syrup
- 1 tsp vanilla extract
- 125 g/4½ oz/heaping ½ cup butter, melted

WHITE CHOCOLATE TOPPING

- 100 g/3½ oz white chocolate, chopped
- 1 tbsp almond oil
- 50 g/1¾ oz/scant ½ cup royal icing (confectioners') sugar, sifted
- 1 tbsp cinnamon sugar or cocoa powder, for dusting
- 12 chocolate-coated coffee beans

Preheat the oven to 180°C/350°F/Gas 4. Line a 12-cup muffin pan with paper muffin cases.

Put the hazelnuts, sugar, tapioca flour, espresso, baking powder, eggs, milk, hazelnut syrup and vanilla into a bowl and beat with an electric mixer, starting at slow speed and gradually increasing the speed to high. Add the melted butter and beat again. The mixture will be dark brown and quite thin.

Spoon the mixture into the paper cases, filling them three-quarters full. Bake for 18–20 minutes, until springy to the touch. Lift the cakes out of the tin and leave to cool on a rack.

To make the topping, melt the white chocolate with almond oil in a heatproof bowl set over a saucepan of gently simmering water, stirring until smooth (or in the microwave, but take care as white chocolate burns easily). Add the icing sugar and stir well, until creamy and spreadable. Spoon the topping over each cooled cake, smooth it down, then sift over a little cinnamon sugar or cocoa powder and top with a chocolate-coated coffee bean.

For extra 'ooh-la-la'

For utterly decadent cupcakes, half-fill the paper cases with the cake mixture, pop a blob of hazelnut butter (see page 42) into the centre of each cake, then cover with more mixture before baking.

Cornbread and red pepper muffins

makes: 12 muffins
health: gluten-free
cook: 38 minutes
store: best eaten on same day; 2 days in airtight container. Freeze well
compost: eggshells, pepper trimmings

200 ml/7 fl oz/scant 1 cup olive oil, plus extra for brushing
250 g/9 oz/2 cups polenta
1½ tsp gluten-free baking powder
1½ tsp guar gum
1 tsp dried oregano
1 tsp hot chilli powder
1 tsp cracked black pepper
½ tsp salt
ground dried chilli flakes, to taste
2 eggs
200 ml/7 fl oz/scant 1 cup whole milk
100 g/3½ oz mature Cheddar, grated
50 g/1¾ oz Parmesan, grated
3 tbsp chopped fresh basil leaves

ROASTED RED (BELL) PEPPERS

2 red (bell) peppers (250 g/9 oz), deseeded and chopped into 1 cm/½ in pieces
1–2 tbsp olive oil
1 tsp dried oregano

TOPPING

25 g/1 oz Parmesan, finely grated
dried chilli flakes, for grinding

While we were tweaking the recipes for this book, Charlotte and I were baking like whirling dervishes. One morning we had a pile of these cheerful red-and-yellow muffins on the counter when 2 hungry chaps arrived to deliver a new oven. Dave and Doug loved these muffins and felt they would be great with home-made guacamole. They were right.

Preheat the oven to 180°C/350°F/Gas 4. Brush a 12-cup bendy silicone muffin pan with olive oil and place on a metal baking sheet.

For the roasted red peppers, put the peppers in a roasting pan and sprinkle with the olive oil and oregano. Roast for 20 minutes. Weigh out 150 g/5½ oz of the peppers for the muffin mixture and set the rest aside, covered.

Put the polenta, baking powder, guar gum, oregano, chilli powder, black pepper, salt and chilli flakes into a mixing bowl and mix with a fork.

Crack the eggs into a large mixing bowl. Add the milk, olive oil, Cheddar, Parmesan and basil and beat with an electric mixer at high speed until combined. Add the 150 g/5½ oz roasted peppers and stir in using a rubber spatula.

Add the dry ingredients to the wet and, using a rubber spatula, mix in quickly – just until all the ingredients are combined. Scrape down the sides of the bowl to ensure everything is mixed in, but don't overmix.

Spoon the mixture into the muffin cups. If you have any spare roasted pepper pieces, pop them on top and sprinkle with finely grated Parmesan. Finally, grind chilli flakes over each muffin, to taste.

Bake for 18 minutes, until gently domed and springy to the touch. They'll be a lovely golden colour when ready. Leave for 2–3 minutes, then carefully turn out onto a rack.

For extra 'ooh-la-la'

Fill the muffins with chilli jam; half-fill the muffin cups, add ½ tsp chilli jam to each, then cover with more mixture before baking.

traybakes

Little Em's summer berry cake

makes: 15 pieces
health: gluten-free
cook: 22 minutes
store: best eaten on same day. 3 days in fridge. Freeze well
compost: eggshells, spare lemon bits

This is super-swift and simple to bake. It can be made with whatever berries are in season or use up spare fruit from the freezer.

- 250 g/9 oz/scant 1¼ cups butter, melted, plus extra for brushing
- 4 eggs
- 2 egg yolks
- 185 g/6½ oz/scant 1 cup light brown sugar
- 100 g/3½ oz/1 cup ground almonds
- 100 g/3½ oz/generous ¾ cup polenta
- 75 g/2¾ oz tapioca flour
- 1½ tsp gluten-free baking powder
- 1½ tsp guar gum
- 1 tsp vanilla extract
- ½ tsp salt
- grated zest of 2 unwaxed lemons
- 225 g/8 oz/2 cups mixed summer berries (such as redcurrants, blackcurrants, blackberries, raspberries)

TOPPING

- 50 g/1¾ oz/¼ cup caster (superfine) sugar
- 100 ml/3½ fl oz/⅓ cup lemon juice
- 6 sugar cubes

Preheat the oven to 180°C/350°F/Gas 4. Cut a rectangle of baking parchment to line the bottom of a 30 x 23 x 4 cm/12 x 9 x 1½ in baking tin. Brush the tin liberally with melted butter before popping in the baking parchment.

Put the melted butter into a large mixing bowl with the eggs, yolks, sugar, almonds, polenta, tapioca flour, baking powder, guar gum, vanilla extract, salt and lemon zest. Beat with an electric mixer until creamy, then stir in the berries.

Pour the mixture into the tin and smooth over with a spatula. Bake for 22 minutes, until the surface springs back when pressed with your fingertips. Leave in the tin to cool slightly while you make the topping.

To make the topping, stir the caster sugar and lemon juice together over a low heat until the sugar dissolves. Roughly crush or crumble the sugar cubes into the mixture.

Pierce the cake all over with a skewer while still warm and pour the topping mixture over it. The syrup will soak in and the crushed sugar cubes will rest on the top. Leave in the tin to cool completely, then turn out on to a rack and cut into pieces.

Make the most of your freezer

You can use frozen fruits, but thaw them first, otherwise they'll freeze your mixture, making it hard to work with and less likely to rise well.

Fig, honey and Greek yogurt cake

100 g/3½ oz/scant ½ cup butter, softened, plus extra, melted, for brushing
tapioca flour, for dusting
4 eggs
150 g/5½ oz clear honey
100 g/3½ oz/7 tbsp Greek yogurt or crème fraîche
100 ml/3½ fl oz whole milk
1 tsp vanilla extract
200 g/7 oz dried figs, chopped
100 g/3½ oz/generous ¾ cup pistachios, toasted and chopped
85 g/3 oz/scant 1 cup ground almonds
70 g/2½ oz/generous ½ cup polenta
50 g/1¾ oz/5 tbsp ground brown flax seeds (linseed)
1½ tsp guar gum
1½ tsp gluten-free baking powder
8 fresh figs
3 tbsp clear honey, for drizzling

This is perfect for popping onto the table for everyone to help themselves. The ground flax seeds (linseed) lend a nutty sweetness without making the cake heavy or 'wholemeal'.

Preheat the oven to 180°C/350°F/Gas 4. Brush a 30 x 23 x 4 cm/12 x 9 x 1½ in baking tin with melted butter and dust liberally with tapioca flour.

Put the softened butter into a large mixing bowl. Add the eggs, honey, yogurt, milk and vanilla and beat with an electric mixer until combined.

Put the dried figs, pistachios, almonds, polenta, ground flax seeds, guar gum and baking powder into a large bowl and stir with a fork. Add the egg mixture to the dry ingredients and mix in with a rubber spatula.

Pour the mixture into the tin; it doesn't need to be super-smooth. Cut the fresh figs in half and pop them on top of the mixture, cut-side-up. (Imagine the cake cut into portions, with a fig half on each portion.) Bake for 20–22 minutes, until light golden and the surface springs back when pressed with your fingertips.

Pierce the cake all over with a skewer while still warm and drizzle with honey. (If you first warm the honey gently in the microwave it will be easy to drizzle.) Cut into pieces.

makes: 15 pieces
health: gluten-free
cook: 20–22 minutes
store: best eaten on same day, warm from the oven. Freeze well
compost: eggshells

Make it go further...

Serve warm, with warmed honey drizzled over the top and pistachio ice cream on the side.

Gay's orange cake

makes: 15 pieces
health: gluten-free, dairy-free
cook: 2 hours
store: 3 days in airtight tin well wrapped in clingfilm (plastic wrap). Freeze well
compost: eggshells

2 oranges
melted butter, for brushing
6 eggs
250 g/9 oz/2½ cups ground almonds
250 g/9 oz/1¼ cups granulated sugar
1 tsp gluten-free baking powder

ORANGE CRUNCH TOPPING

8 tbsp granulated sugar
2 tsp orange oil

Gay worked with us for many years; now retired, she continues to be a very wise and special friend. This cake has it all – pure and simple ingredients and reliably delicious results every time.

Wash the oranges and boil them in a pan of water for about 1½ hours, or until very tender – make sure the pan is kept topped up with boiling water. Drain and cool, then blitz to a pulp in a food processor.

Preheat the oven to 180°C/350°F/Gas 4. Cut a rectangle of baking parchment to line the bottom of a 30 x 23 x 4 cm/12 x 9 x 1½ in baking tin. Brush the tin liberally with melted butter before popping in the baking parchment.

Crack the eggs into a large mixing bowl and beat with an electric mixer until frothy. Carefully fold in the almonds, sugar, baking powder and orange pulp.

Pour the mixture into the baking tin and smooth over with a rubber spatula. Bake for 20 minutes, then check and turn the cake around in the oven so it cooks evenly. Bake for a further 10 minutes, until the surface springs back when pressed with your fingertips. Leave in the tin to cool completely, then turn out on to a rack and peel off the baking parchment.

To make the orange crunch topping, put the sugar into a saucepan over a low heat and stir continuously until it dissolves and turns golden brown; take care not to burn it. Carefully stir in the orange oil – the sugar will spit and smoke a little. Take the pan off the heat. Using a metal spoon, drizzle the sugar over the cake. You need to work quickly, as the sugar will start to set almost immediately. Cut into pieces.

Make it go further...

Serve warm as a pudding with crème fraîche and a dollop of warm orange marmalade or curd on the side.

Almond moon (cherry and almond slices)

makes: 15 pieces
health: gluten-free
cook: 55 minutes
store: 5 days in airtight tin. Freeze well
compost: eggshells, cherry stones and stalks

This is our take on the familiar British Bakewell tart. Instead of pastry we use our classic polenta shortbread base, packed with almonds. The Drunken cherry filling is strictly for grown-ups, and the topping is a simple frangipane with cherries stirred in.

Polenta shortbread base (see page 83)

FRANGIPANE

3 eggs

175 g/6 oz/generous ¾ cup vanilla granulated sugar

140 g/5 oz/1½ cups ground almonds

1½ tsp almond extract

100 g/3½ oz/generous ½ cup ground brown flax seeds (linseed)

140 g/5 oz dried sour cherries

175 g/6 oz/¾ cup butter, melted

FILLING

2 tbsp cherry jam

125 g/4½ oz Drunken cherries (see page 84), pitted

TOPPING

55 g/2 oz/scant ½ cup almonds, toasted and roughly chopped

70 g/2½ oz dried sour cherries

Preheat the oven to 180°C/350°F/Gas 4. Prepare and bake the polenta shortbread base (see page 83).

To make the frangipane, crack the eggs into a large mixing bowl. Add the sugar, almonds, almond extract, ground flax seeds, sour cherries and melted butter. Beat with an electric mixer, starting at low speed and gradually increasing to high, until fluffy and creamy, but don't overmix.

Once the shortbread base has cooled, spread the cherry jam evenly over it. Scatter the Drunken cherries over the jam.

Spoon the frangipane mixture over the cherries and jam, spreading evenly while being careful not to mix it with the jam and fruit.

Sprinkle the top with the chopped almonds and sour cherries, pushing them in lightly with your hands. Bake for 35 minutes, until deep golden and firm to the touch. Leave in the tin to cool completely, then turn out and cut into pieces.

Great for kids

To make a non-alcoholic version, use sour cherries rather than Drunken cherries in the filling.

Baking tip

For this recipe you don't need to wait 2–3 months for the Drunken cherries; a week is fine.

Sticky toffee-apple shortbread

makes: 15 pieces
health: gluten-free
cook: 50 minutes
store: 2–3 days in fridge. Freeze well
compost: eggshells, apple trimmings

I remember the excitement of our family Bonfire Night party, although many of my memories centre on the food rather than the fireworks – simple buttered jacket potatoes with beans and cheese and home-made toffee apples. The challenge was to convert the toffee apple taste into cake form. This makes a great slice for an afternoon tea break or a fab pudding served warm with crème fraîche and a cheeky splash of cider brandy.

Cornflour shortbread base (see page 82)

BAKED APPLES

300 g/10½ oz cooking apples
2 tbsp cider brandy or Calvados
1 tbsp light brown sugar
4 tbsp good-quality apple sauce
50 g/1¾ oz/5 tbsp plump raisins
1 tsp ground cinnamon
grated zest of 1 unwaxed lemon

CRUMBLE TOPPING

100 g/3½ oz/scant ½ cup butter, chilled and cubed
140 g/5 oz/scant ¾ cup granulated sugar
140 g/5 oz gluten-free oat flour
100 g/3½ oz/1¼ cups gluten-free oats

SYRUP TOPPING

15 g/½ oz/1 tbsp butter, melted
1 egg
60 g/2¼ oz/5 tbsp light brown sugar
25 g/1 oz golden syrup

Preheat the oven to 180°C/350°F/Gas 4. Prepare and bake the cornflour shortbread base (see page 82); leave until completely cool.

Meanwhile, to make the baked apples, core the apples and chop into roughly 1 cm/½ in chunks. Place in a baking tin and stir in the cider brandy and sugar. Bake for about 15 minutes, stirring after 7 minutes. Allow to cool.

Place the apple sauce, raisins, cinnamon and lemon zest in a bowl, add the cooled baked apple mixture and stir well. Set aside.

To make the crumble topping, put the butter, sugar, oat flour and oats into a bowl. Rub the mixture between your fingers to break up the butter, then beat with an electric mixer at slow speed until you have a clumpy crumble texture.

To make the syrup topping, put the melted butter into a bowl with the egg, sugar and golden syrup and beat with a whisk until well combined.

Spread the baked apple mixture over the shortbread base using a palette knife. Press the mixture to make an even layer, making sure it fills the corners. Sprinkle the crumble evenly over the apple and press firmly but gently all over. Drizzle the syrup over the top. Bake for 35 minutes, until the top is a deep golden colour. The sides should also be golden: to check, push the cake away from the edge of the tin with a palette knife and have a peek. Cut into pieces. This can be served either warm or cold.

Great for kids

Replace the cider brandy with apple juice for a non-alcoholic version.

Ginger and apricot slices

melted butter, for brushing
350 g/12 oz/2⅔ cups dried apricots, chopped
115 g/4 oz/generous ½ cup granulated sugar
50 g/1¾ oz stem ginger in syrup (drained weight)

CRUMBLE

200 g/7 oz/scant 1 cup butter, chilled and cubed
150 g/5½ oz/¾ cup light brown sugar, plus 1 tbsp for sprinkling
150 g/5½ oz/generous 1 cup almonds, toasted and chopped
140 g/5 oz/generous 1 cup polenta
115 g/4 oz/scant 1½ cups gluten-free oats
70 g/2½ oz/¾ cup ground almonds
3 tsp ground ginger

makes: 15 pieces
health: gluten-free
cook: 35–40 minutes
store: 5 days in airtight tin. Freeze well
compost: eggshells

This fruity number tastes gorgeous. We bake it, pop it out on the counter, listen to people say they're not keen on ginger… and it is gone. Amazing. Cut into squares and wrapped in foil (to keep the crumble in place), it's a great addition to a packed lunch box.

Preheat the oven to 180°C/350°F/Gas 4. Cut a rectangle of baking parchment to line the bottom of a 30 x 23 x 4 cm/12 x 9 x 1½ in baking tin. Brush the tin liberally with melted butter before popping in the baking parchment.

Put the apricots, sugar and 100 ml/8 fl oz/scant 1 cup water into a saucepan and cook over a medium-low heat for about 8–10 minutes, until thick and jammy, stirring regularly to prevent it from sticking. Crush the stem ginger in a food processor or blender, then stir into the apricot mixture. Set aside to let the apricots absorb all of the liquid.

Put all the crumble ingredients into a large mixing bowl. Rub the mixture between your fingers to break up the butter, then beat with an electric mixer at low speed until the mixture forms a clumpy crumble texture.

Press half the crumble mixture firmly into the baking tin. Press down with the back of a spoon to form a solid, even base. Spread the jammy apricot mixture over the crumble base, taking care to leave the crumble undisturbed.

Press the remaining crumble lightly over the apricot mixture, then sprinkle 1 tbsp brown sugar over the top. Bake for 35–40 minutes, until the top and sides are a deep golden colour and the filling looks darker. To check, push the cake away from the edge of the tin with a palette knife and have a peek. Cut into pieces.

Make it go further…

Mix the ginger syrup with some custard (see page 147) and serve this as a pudding.

Snowy Hills (lemon and ginger slices)

Polenta shortbread base (see page 83), made with 1 tbsp ground ginger
2 eggs
125 g/4½ oz/1¼ cups ground almonds
140 g/5 oz/scant ¾ cup brown vanilla sugar
1 tsp gluten-free baking powder
85 g/3 oz/scant ¾ cup polenta
4 tbsp good-quality lemon curd
grated zest of 2 unwaxed lemons
1 tbsp lemon juice
2 tsp lemon oil
140 g/5 oz/scant ¾ cup butter, melted
light brown sugar, for sprinkling

As I write these recipes I realise how many of our cakes are inspired by rambles in the countryside. The baking powder in this recipe needs to be 'sandwiched' between the other dry ingredients to prevent it from reacting with the lemon juice, which can cause the mixture to separate.

Preheat the oven to 180°C/350°F/Gas 4. Prepare and bake the polenta shortbread base (see page 83), adding the ground ginger to the mixture.

Crack the eggs into a large mixing bowl. Add the almonds, sugar, baking powder, polenta and 1 tbsp of the lemon curd.

Mix the lemon zest, juice and oil with the melted butter and then add it to the egg-and-almond mixture. Beat with an electric mixer at high speed until smooth.

Once the shortbread base has cooled, spread the remaining 3 tbsp lemon curd evenly over it. Spoon the cake mixture on top of the curd, spreading it evenly and being careful not to mix it with the curd. Bake for 25 minutes, until golden brown and the surface springs back when pressed with your fingertips.

Leave in the tin to cool completely. Sprinkle the top of the cake with brown sugar, then slide it out of the tin and cut into pieces.

makes: 15 pieces
health: gluten-free
cook: 40 minutes for the base
store: 5 days in airtight tin. Freezes well
compost: eggshells, spare lemon

Make it go further...

Serve warm, with ice cream on the side.

Absolutely almond cake

makes: 30 pieces
health: gluten-free
cook: 30–32 minutes
store: 5 days in airtight tin. Freezes well
compost: eggshell

- 250 g/9 oz/generous 1 cup butter, melted, plus extra for brushing
- 400 g/14 oz marzipan
- 4 eggs
- 350 g/12 oz/3½ cups ground almonds
- 225 g/8 oz/generous 1 cup granulated sugar
- 4 tsp almond extract
- 50 g/1¾ oz/⅓ cup almonds, roughly chopped

This is heaven for almond fans – you can also make it with ground pistachios if you prefer. Best served in very small squares and ideally accompanying an espresso to balance the sweetness.

Preheat the oven to 180°C/350°F/Gas 4. Cut a rectangle of baking parchment to line the bottom of a 30 x 23 x 4 cm/12 x 9 x 1½ in baking tin. Brush the tin liberally with melted butter before popping in the baking parchment.

Knead the marzipan to soften it. Roll it between 2 pieces of baking parchment to fit the baking tin. Set aside.

Put the eggs into a large mixing bowl. Add the ground almonds, sugar and almond extract, then add the melted butter. Beat with an electric mixer at high speed until smooth and creamy.

Pour half of the mixture into the tin, and smooth over with a palette knife. Gently place the rolled out marzipan on top. Pour over the remaining cake mixture and smooth over, taking care to cover the marzipan completely. Sprinkle the chopped almonds over the top.

Bake for 30–32 minutes, until the top and sides are a light golden colour. To check, push the cake away from the edge of the tin with a palette knife and have a peek. Cut into pieces. This can either be served warm or cold.

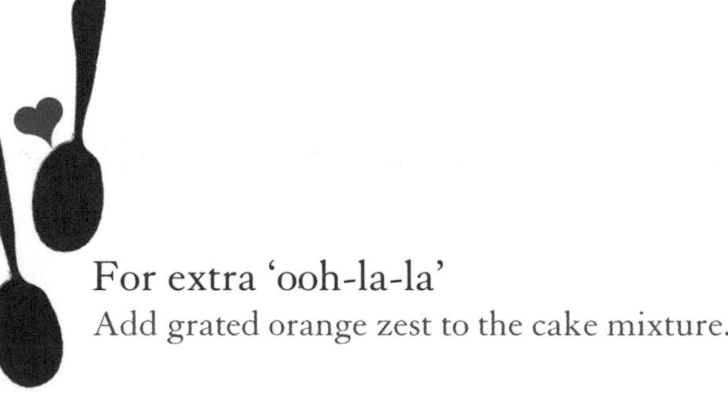

For extra 'ooh-la-la'

Add grated orange zest to the cake mixture.

Papa Haydn's pecan pie

Cornflour shortbread base (see page 82)
25 g/1 oz/2 tbsp butter, melted
250 g/9 oz/1¼ cups light brown sugar
150 g/5½ oz golden syrup
grated zest of 1 unwaxed lemon
3 eggs
225 g/8 oz/2¼ cups pecan halves, toasted

This was inspired by wonderful Thanksgiving suppers cooked by my American cousin, Diana. The original contained bourbon and wheat flour and was stupendously good. This is a gluten-free, sober version that we think you might just fall in love with.

Preheat the oven to 180°C/350°F/Gas 4. Prepare and bake the cornflour shortbread base (see page 82). Allow to cool completely.

Put the melted butter into a large mixing bowl with the sugar, golden syrup, lemon zest and eggs. Beat with a whisk until combined. Set aside.

Spread the pecans evenly over the shortbread base. Carefully pour the syrup mixture over the top.

Bake for 20 minutes, then cover with a piece of baking parchment to prevent the edges from browning too much and bake for a further 10–15 minutes, until the syrup in the middle is completely set. Leave in the tin to cool.

makes: 1 x 30 x 23 cm/
12 x 9 in pie
health: gluten-free
cook: 45–50 minutes
store: 5 days in airtight tin
compost: eggshells

Make it go further...

Serve warm, with ice cream on the side.

Squillionaire's shortbread

makes: 15 pieces
health: gluten-free
cook: 20 minutes
store: 7 days in airtight tin. Freezes well
compost: eggshell

Polenta shortbread base (see page 83)
300 g/10½ oz dulce de leche
250 g/9 oz dark chocolate, cut into chunks
40 g/1½ oz/3 tbsp butter
cocoa powder, for dusting

Millionaire's shortbread is a classic of the British biscuit tin. Squillionaire's status is assured by the inclusion of chunks of chocolate as well as a layer of smooth, shiny dark chocolate.

Preheat the oven to 180°C/350°F/Gas 4. Prepare and bake the polenta shortbread base (see page 83). Allow to cool.

Spread the dulce de leche over the base, making sure it is evenly spread right to the edges. Sprinkle about 55 g/2 oz of the chocolate chunks over the caramel and press them in lightly.

Melt the remaining chocolate with the butter in a heatproof bowl set over a saucepan of gently simmering water, stirring until smooth (or in a microwave). Pour this over the caramel base, tipping it gently from side to side so that the chocolate mixture is evenly spread to the edges of the tin. Leave in the tin to cool, dust with cocoa powder lightly and evenly, then place in the fridge to chill. Cut into pieces.

For a quick and easy birthday cake

Make a stack of squares and scatter with chocolate 'gold coins' for a lovely, quirky birthday 'cake'.

Congo bars

makes: 15 pieces
health: gluten-free
cook: 20 minutes
store: 7 days in airtight tin
compost: eggshells

Polenta shortbread base (see page 83)
300 g/10½ oz dulce de leche
200 g/7 oz/1 cup pecan halves, toasted and cooled
25 g/1 oz coconut chips, toasted and cooled
100 g/3½ oz milk chocolate buttons
cocoa powder, for dusting

This nutty shortbread topped with nuts and chocolate is one of our best-selling products. It's worth the slight kerfuffle of pre-toasting the pecans and coconut, as this brings a lovely smokiness to the party.

Preheat the oven to 180°C/350°F/Gas 4. Prepare and bake the polenta shortbread base (see page 83). Allow to cool completely.

Spread the dulce de leche over the base, making sure it is evenly spread right to the edges. Sprinkle the toasted pecans evenly over the caramel. Sprinkle on the toasted coconut chips and push them gently into the caramel. Sprinkle on the chocolate buttons, making sure they are evenly distributed.

Pop into the oven for 1–2 minutes, so the chocolate melts very slightly – the idea is just to make it stick.

Allow to cool. When the chocolate buttons are almost reset back to their original form, but still slightly tacky to the touch, dust lightly and evenly with cocoa powder. Place in the fridge to chill. Once chilled, remove from the tin and cut into pieces.

For a grown-up treat

Dark chocolate chunks are lovely in place of the chocolate buttons.

Cornflour shortbread base

200 g/7 oz/scant 1 cup butter, chilled and cubed, plus extra, melted, for brushing
90 g/3¼ oz/¾ cup icing (confectioners') sugar
90 g/3¼ oz/generous ½ cup cornflour (cornstarch)
90 g/3¼ oz/generous ½ cup brown rice flour
60 g/2¼ oz/⅔ cup ground almonds
25 g/1 oz sorghum flour
tapioca flour, for dusting

Preheat the oven to 180°C/350°F/Gas 4. Brush a 30 x 23 x 4 cm/12 x 9 x 1½ in baking tin liberally with melted butter.

Put the butter, icing sugar, cornflour, rice flour, almonds and sorghum flour into a food processor and whizz until you have a soft, sticky but pliable dough.

Cut 2 sheets of baking parchment to the size of the baking tin plus a generous margin. Dust your hands, work surface and rolling pin liberally with tapioca flour. Roll out the dough between the 2 sheets of parchment until it is the size of the tin. Peel off the top layer of parchment. Carefully transfer the rolled dough, still on the parchment, into the tin.

Bake for 15 minutes, until golden and quite firm to the touch. Leave in the tin to cool completely.

Make the most of your freezer

Make 2–3 bases and freeze them, raw or baked.

Polenta shortbread base

- 125 g/4½ oz/generous ½ cup butter, softened and cubed, plus extra, melted, for brushing
- 140 g/5 oz/generous 1 cup polenta
- 125 g/4½ oz/generous ½ cup brown vanilla sugar
- 70 g/2½ oz/scant 1 cup ground hazelnuts
- 100 g/3½ oz/1 cup ground almonds
- 40 g/1½ oz/5 tbsp almonds, toasted and chopped
- 1 egg

Preheat the oven to 180°C/350°F/Gas 4. Cut a rectangle of baking parchment to line the bottom of a 30 x 23 x 4 cm/12 x 9 x 1½ in baking tin. Brush it and the tin liberally with melted butter before popping in the parchment.

Put the butter, polenta, sugar, hazelnuts, ground almonds, chopped almonds and egg into a mixing bowl and beat with an electric mixer until the mixture forms a soft but fairly grainy dough.

Press the mixture into the baking tin with your hands and smooth down with the back of a large spoon, making sure it is evenly spread.

Bake for 20 minutes, until golden and quite firm to the touch. Leave in the tin to cool completely.

Make the most of your freezer

Make 2–3 bases and freeze them, raw or baked.

Drunken cherries

450 g/1 lb cherries, destalked
225 g/8 oz/generous 1 cup granulated sugar
200 ml/7 fl oz/scant 1 cup good French brandy or cherry brandy

Use these to make Almond moon (see page 68), our adult version of a Bakewell tart. Or serve them with good-quality vanilla ice cream. These quantities are for a 500 ml/18 fl oz/generous 2 cup kilner jar.

Preheat the oven to 200°C/400°F/Gas 6. Sterilize a 500 ml/18 fl oz kilner or screw-top jar. Wash it in hot soapy water, then rinse it in hot water and allow it to drain. Remove any rubber seals and lids and put them into a saucepan of boiling water. Boil hard for 5 minutes, then drain and lay them on kitchen paper to dry.

Put the washed jar on a clean baking sheet and place in the oven for 10 minutes. Remove from the oven and allow to cool.

Spoon the prepared cherries into the jar, layering them with the sugar. Fill the jar to the top with cherries, but stop the sugar layers about three-quarters of the way up, then fill to the top with brandy or cherry brandy.

Put the rubber seals back on and seal, making sure the lid is on firmly. Store in a cool, dark place. Your cherries will be ready to enjoy in 2–3 months' time.

Almond praline

55 g/2 oz/generous ½ cup almonds, roughly chopped
90 g/3¼ oz/scant ½ cup granulated sugar

Cover a baking sheet with baking parchment. Put the almonds and sugar into a small saucepan over a low heat. Stir continuously until the sugar has dissolved and formed a golden liquid coating the almonds. Take great care as the liquid is extremely hot.

Pour the mixture onto the baking sheet. Leave to set and cool completely.

Break up the praline into chunks and, if you wish, blitz it in the food processor until it is as fine as you need it to be.

brownies and other chocolatey things

Heathcliff brownies

makes: 1 x 30 x 23 cm/
12 x 9 in cake
health: gluten-free
cook: 25–28 minutes
store: 10 days in airtight tin.
Freezes well
compost: eggshells

175 g/6 oz/¾ cup butter, plus extra, melted, for brushing
400 g/14 oz dark chocolate, chopped
1 tsp espresso coffee powder or granules, dissolved in 1–2 tsp hot water
finely grated zest of 1 orange
1 tsp orange oil
4 eggs
100 g/3½ oz/1 cup ground almonds
125 g/4½ oz milk chocolate, chopped
150 g/5½ oz/¾ cup muscovado sugar
85 g/3 oz/generous ½ cup almonds, toasted and chopped
pinch of salt
2 drops of vanilla extract

TOPPING

250 g/9 oz dark chocolate, cut into chunks
1 tbsp olive oil
1 tsp orange oil

Like the romantic hero of 'Wuthering Heights', these brownies are dark and brooding. They're flavoured with orange and just sweet enough, with lots of body and bite. Delicious served slightly chilled and cut into thin slices, but equally good warmed through and served with clotted cream and/or ice cream, they are the ultimate in sinful puddings.

Preheat the oven to 180°C/350°F/Gas 4. Cut a rectangle of baking parchment to line the bottom of a 30 x 23 x 4 cm/12 x 9 x 1½ in baking tin. Pop the parchment into the tin and brush it and the tin with melted butter.

Melt the butter with 200 g/7 oz of the dark chocolate in a heatproof bowl set over a saucepan of gently simmering water, stirring until smooth (or in a microwave). Stir in the coffee. Allow the mixture to cool slightly and then stir in the orange zest and orange oil.

Crack the eggs into a mixing bowl, then add the ground almonds, milk chocolate chunks and the remaining 200 g/7 oz of dark chocolate, the sugar, chopped almonds, salt and vanilla. Finally, pour in the melted butter-and-chocolate mixture. Using an electric mixer, beat at medium speed until creamy and thickened, but don't overmix as too much air will cause the brownie to crumble when baked.

Spoon the mixture into the tin and bake for 25–28 minutes. Take care not to overbake. The brownie is ready when the edges are slightly crusty and the middle is still soft, but with a firmish 'skin'. Allow to cool for 1 hour.

For the topping, melt 150 g/5½ oz of the chocolate with the olive oil and orange oil in a heatproof bowl set over a saucepan of gently simmering water, stirring until smooth (or in a microwave). Spread this over the brownie. Scatter the remaining 100 g/3½ oz of chocolate over the top and leave to set for 2 hours. Cut into pieces.

Great for kids

Use 100 g/3½ oz dark chocolate buttons for decorating, instead of rough chunks.

Skipper's brownies

makes: 15 pieces
health: gluten-free
cook: 25 minutes
store: 7 days in airtight container. Freeze well
compost: eggshells

175 g/6 oz/¾ cup butter, plus extra, melted, for brushing
200 g/7 oz dark chocolate, chopped
100 g/3½ oz/generous ½ cup raisins
3 tbsp good-quality dark rum
4 eggs
275 g/9¾ oz milk chocolate, cut into chunks
150 g/5½ oz/¾ cup granulated sugar
1 tsp gluten-free baking powder
100 g/3½ oz/1¼ cups walnuts, ground
75 g/2¾ oz/generous ½ cup walnut pieces, toasted
1 tsp vanilla extract
pinch of salt

TOPPING

50 g/1¾ oz/5 tbsp raisins
4 tsp good-quality dark rum
25 g/1 oz/2 tbsp butter
100 g/3½ oz milk chocolate, chopped

This is my homage to my rather hard-drinking trawlermen uncles, Old Navy rum being one of their favourite tipples. If you toast the walnuts you'll achieve a smokiness of flavour that goes tickety boo with the rum.

Preheat the oven to 180°C/350°F/Gas 4. Cut a rectangle of baking parchment to line the bottom of a 30 x 23 x 4 cm/12 x 9 x 1½ in baking tin. Pop the parchment in the tin and brush the parchment and the tin with melted butter.

Melt the butter with the dark chocolate in a heatproof bowl set over a saucepan of gently simmering water, stirring until smooth (or in a microwave).

Put the raisins in a small saucepan and pour the rum over. Heat gently for 1 minute, then set aside.

Crack the eggs into a mixing bowl and add the milk chocolate chunks, sugar, baking powder, ground walnuts, walnut pieces, vanilla and salt. Add the rum-soaked raisins and melted butter-and-chocolate mixture. Using an electric mixer, beat at medium speed until pale and slightly thicker.

Spoon the mixture into the tin and bake for 25 minutes. When ready, the cake should spring back when pressed gently with your fingertips, but will have a soft, fudgy, brownie-like texture. Leave in the tin to cool.

For the topping, gently heat the raisins in the rum in a small saucepan, then blitz to a paste in a food processor. Melt the butter with the chocolate in a heatproof bowl set over a saucepan of gently simmering water, stirring until smooth (or in a microwave). Stir in the rum-and-raisin mixture. Spoon the mixture over the cooled brownie, spreading evenly. Allow the topping to set before removing it from the tin and cutting into portions.

For extra 'ooh-la-la'

For an ultra-decadent brownie, while still warm from the oven you could pierce all over and drizzle with 1–2 tbsp rum before adding the topping.

A very chocolatey cake

150 g/5½ oz/scant ¾ cup butter, plus extra, melted, for brushing
200 g/7 oz dark chocolate, chopped
5 eggs
200 g/7 oz/1 cup granulated sugar
1 tsp gluten-free baking powder
100 g/3½ oz/1 cup ground almonds
60 g/2¼ oz/6 tbsp ground brown flax seeds (linseed)
½ tsp vanilla extract
100 g/3½ oz milk chocolate, cut into chunks

TOPPING

50 g/1¾ oz/4 tbsp butter
100 g/3½ oz dark chocolate, cut into chunks

makes: 1 x 23 cm/9 in round cake
health: gluten-free
cook: 30–35 minutes
store: 7 days in airtight tin. Freezes well
compost: eggshells

This simple cake can be made in a shallow baking tin or as a round cake. It is velvety smooth and moist. It can be left undecorated or you can smother it with a decadent ganache.

Preheat the oven to 180°C/350°F/Gas 4. Line a 23 cm/9 in round springform tin (or a 30 x 23 x 4 cm/12 x 9 x 1½ in baking tin) with baking parchment, then brush with melted butter.

Melt the butter with the dark chocolate in a heatproof bowl set over a saucepan of gently simmering water, stirring until smooth (or in a microwave).

Crack the eggs into a mixing bowl, then add the sugar, baking powder, almonds, flax seeds and vanilla. Pour in the melted butter-and-chocolate mixture. Using an electric mixer, beat at medium speed until creamy, then fold in the milk chocolate chunks with a rubber spatula.

Pour the mixture into the tin and place on a metal baking sheet. Bake for 30 minutes (20–25 if using a rectangular tin), then check and cover the top with baking parchment if the cake needs to be cooked for longer. When ready, the cake should spring back when pressed gently with your fingertips, but will have a soft, fudgy, brownie-like texture. Leave in the tin on a rack for 1 hour.

For the topping, melt the butter with the chocolate in a heatproof bowl set over a saucepan of gently simmering water, stirring until smooth (or in a microwave). Turn the cake out onto a rack and peel off the baking parchment. Spread the chocolate-and-butter mixture over it, using a palette knife. Leave to set for about 2 hours.

For a big party

Double the ingredients and divide the mixture between 3 x 20 cm/8 in shallow cake tins. Reduce the baking time by 5 minutes. Add chocolate cream filling (see page 126) in between each layer.

Chocolate and prune cakes

makes: 12 squares or rounds
health: gluten-free
cook: 35–40 minutes
store: 7 days in airtight container. Freeze well
compost: eggshells

After a fantastic cycling and camping holiday in the Agen region of South-West France, I returned home keen to devise a recipe using the stunning pruneaux d'Agen that we had feasted on. These were sold at farm gates, alongside superlatively good Armagnacs. This cake is not too sweet and perfect served in thin slivers after supper.

150 g/5½ oz/generous ½ cup butter, plus extra, melted, for brushing
250 g/9 oz/1½ cups pitted prunes, quartered
4 tbsp Armagnac
600 g/1 lb 5 oz milk chocolate, chopped
6 eggs
1 tbsp espresso coffee granules, dissolved in 1 tbsp hot water
200 g/7 oz/2 cups ground almonds
100 g/3½ oz chestnut flour
1 tbsp orange oil
¼ tsp vanilla extract

TOPPING

25 g/1 oz/2 tbsp butter
50 g/1¾ oz dark chocolate, chopped
12 pitted prunes

Preheat the oven to 170°C/325°F/Gas 3. Brush a 30 x 23 x 4 cm/12 x 9 x 1½ in baking tin with melted butter.

Put the prunes in a small pan, pour the Armagnac over and heat gently for a minute or 2 then set aside to cool.

Melt the butter with the chocolate in a heatproof bowl set over a saucepan of gently simmering water, stirring until smooth (or in a microwave).

Crack the eggs into a large mixing bowl and add the prunes, Armagnac, coffee, ground almonds, chestnut flour, orange oil and vanilla. Add the melted butter-and-chocolate mixture. Using an electric mixer, beat at high speed until the mixture is creamy and you can see bubbles rising to the surface.

Spoon the mixture into the tin and spread out evenly. Bang the tin firmly on a work surface to get rid of air pockets. Bake for 35–40 minutes, until the surface springs back when pressed gently with your fingertips. A flat cake skewer will come out clean when the cake is ready. Leave to cool in the tin.

For the topping, melt the butter with the chocolate in a heatproof bowl set over a saucepan of gently simmering water, stirring until smooth (or in a microwave). Dip each prune into the chocolate mixture and arrange on the cake. Drizzle the remaining chocolate mixture over the cake if you wish. Slide the cake out of the tin and cut into 12 squares or rounds.

Great for kids

To make a non-alcoholic version, add the chopped prunes without soaking them in Armagnac.

Chocolate puddings with a hint of chilli

makes: 12 puddings
health: gluten-free
cook: 15–17 minutes
store: 2 days in fridge; can be reheated. Freeze well

A fabulously easy pud. We like to call these 'muddy bottom infernos', but they can be as fiery as you like, depending on how much chilli you use. Definitely best eaten hot, straight from the oven.

25 g/1 oz/2 tbsp butter, melted, plus extra for brushing
200 g/7 oz/1 cup granulated sugar
100 g/3½ oz chestnut flour
25 g/1 oz/¼ cup ground almonds
3 tbsp cocoa powder
1 tsp vanilla extract
1 tsp chocolate extract
¼ tsp dried chilli flakes
150 ml/5 fl oz/⅔ cup whole milk
100 g/3½ oz dark chocolate, cut into small chunks

MUDDY BOTTOM TOPPING

60 g/2¼ oz/5 tbsp light brown sugar
2 tbsp cocoa powder
100 ml/3½ fl oz/⅓ cup boiling water

Preheat the oven to 180°C/350°F/Gas 4. Brush a 12-cup silicone muffin pan with melted butter and place on a baking sheet.

Put the sugar, chestnut flour, almonds, cocoa powder, vanilla extract, chocolate extract and chilli flakes in a mixing bowl, then add the melted butter and milk. Using an electric mixer, beat at high speed until smooth and creamy. Stir in the chocolate chunks using a rubber spatula.

Spoon the mixture into the muffin pan, filling the cups to just above halfway.

For the muddy bottom topping, put the sugar and cocoa in a jug, pour in the boiling water and mix with a fork until the cocoa is dissolved. Pour the topping over the mixture in the muffin cups, leaving a little space at the top of each. At this point it looks very wrong – but trust the recipe!

Bake for 15–17 minutes. The cakes will feel quite squishy, due to their muddy bottoms. Leave in the muffin pan to cool slightly, then turn out. Serve warm, or allow to cool and set.

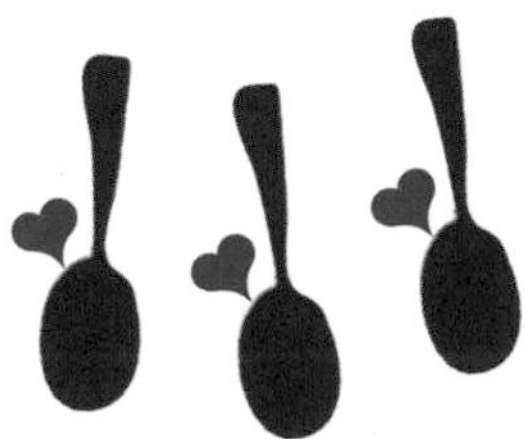

For extra 'ooh-la-la'

Serve with a hot chocolate sauce: heat 100 g/3½ oz dark chocolate chunks with 40 g/1½ oz/3 tbsp butter and 6 tbsp double (heavy) cream in a saucepan over a medium-low heat, stirring, until smooth.

Chockabloc

225 g/8 oz/1 cup butter, plus extra, melted, for brushing
150 g/5½ oz/7 tbsp golden syrup
1 tbsp espresso coffee granules
325 g/11½ oz dark chocolate, chopped
1 tbsp almond oil
1 tsp orange oil
2 tsp mixed spice
400 g/14 oz Amondi cookies (see page 130)
100 g/3½ oz/¾ cup almonds, toasted and chopped

This is our interpretation of the Italian 'panforte'. The Amondi cookie pieces add the required chewiness, while the chocolate mixture melts in the mouth. It's a lovely chocolate-rich treat to serve with coffee after a sumptuous meal. Definitely best served slightly chilled and in very thin slices … you can always come back for more, and bets are on that you will!

Brush a 30 x 23 x 4 cm/12 x 9 x 1½ in baking tin with melted butter.

Melt the butter with the syrup in a saucepan over a medium-low heat; don't let the mixture get too hot. Add the coffee and whisk to dissolve.

Melt the chocolate with the almond oil in a heatproof bowl set over a saucepan of gently simmering water, stirring until smooth (or in a microwave).

Put the melted chocolate and the melted butter-and-syrup mixtures into a mixing bowl. Using an electric mixer, beat until smooth and thickened. Add the orange oil and mixed spice and stir well.

Break up the Amondi cookies into roughly 2 cm/¾ in chunks and put them into a large mixing bowl. Add the almonds, then pour in the melted mixture and stir well, using a rubber spatula, until all the chunks are coated.

Spoon the mixture into the tin. Bang the tin firmly on the work surface and shake from side to side to level the mixture and get it into the corners. Chill for 2–3 hours to set.

makes: 1 x 30 x 23 cm/
12 x 9 in cake
health: gluten-free
cook: 15–18 minutes
store: 7 days in fridge

For extra 'ooh-la-la'

For an uber-deluxe Chockabloc, add toasted pistachios and chopped apricots.

Chocolate orange tiffin

100 g/3½ oz/scant ½ cup butter, melted, plus extra for brushing
1 batch Custard cream biscuits, without the filling (see page 136)
100 g/3½ oz/5 tbsp golden syrup
1 tbsp cocoa powder

ORANGE CREAM FILLING

50 g/1¾ oz/4 tbsp butter, softened
350 g/12 oz/3 cups icing (confectioners') sugar
finely grated zest and juice of 1 orange

TOPPING

250 g/9 oz dark chocolate, chopped
125 g/4½ oz/generous ½ cup butter
⅛ tsp orange oil

makes: 1 x 30 x 23 cm/ 12 x 9 in cake
health: gluten-free
store: 7 days in fridge. Freezes well
compost: eggshell, bits of orange

This is a lovely, super-easy refrigerator cake; it's quite rich, so like a lot of our chocolatey recipes it's good served chilled and cut into small pieces.

Cut a rectangle of baking parchment to line the bottom of a 30 x 23 x 4 cm/ 12 x 9 x 1½ in baking tin. Pop the parchment into the tin and brush it and the tin liberally with melted butter.

Whizz the biscuits in a food processor until they turn into crumbs. Tip them into a large mixing bowl. Add the melted butter, golden syrup and cocoa and mix with a wooden spoon until the butter is absorbed. Spread the mixture evenly in the tin, using the back of a spoon to press down firmly. Chill in the fridge for 1 hour, until set.

Meanwhile, make the orange cream filling. Put the butter into a mixing bowl and sift in the icing sugar. Add the orange zest and juice. Using an electric mixer, beat at low speed until smooth. Chill in the fridge.

For the topping, melt the chocolate, butter and oil in a heatproof bowl set over a saucepan of gently simmering water, stirring until smooth (or in a microwave).

Spread the orange cream filling evenly over the biscuit base. Spoon the melted chocolate mixture over the filling, tipping the tin from side to side so the chocolate spreads evenly to the edges. Return to the fridge to chill for 1 hour.

Loosen the edges of the cake with a palette knife, slide out of the tin and cut into squares.

Give it a twist

Instead of Custard creams you could use Bourbon creams (see page 126).

Mooosh bars

makes: 1 x 30 x 23 cm/ 12 x 9 in cake
health: gluten-free, dairy-free
cook: 50–52 minutes
store: 5 days in airtight container. Freeze well
compost: eggshells, mint trimmings

CHOCOLATE SHORTBREAD BASE

olive oil, for brushing
2 small eggs
125 g/4½ oz/1¼ cups ground almonds
125 g/4½ oz/generous ½ cup light brown sugar
125 g/4½ oz/1 cup polenta
40 g/1½ oz/5 tbsp almonds, toasted and chopped
1 heaped tbsp cocoa powder

TOPPING

215 g/7½ oz dairy-free dark chocolate, chopped
125 ml/4 fl oz/½ cup olive oil
finely grated zest and juice of 1 lime
2 eggs
100 g/3½ oz/1 cup ground almonds
100 g/3½ oz/½ cup granulated sugar
35 g/1¼ oz/4 tbsp polenta
4 fresh mint leaves, chopped (or ½ tsp dried mint)
⅓ tsp peppermint oil
15–20 fresh mint leaves (optional)

A dairy-free chocolate-and-mint slice, with clean, pure flavours.

Preheat the oven to 180°C/350°F/Gas 4. Cut a rectangle of baking parchment to line the bottom of a 30 x 23 x 4 cm/12 x 9 x 1½ in baking tin. Brush the tin with olive oil and line with the baking parchment.

For the chocolate shortbread base, crack the eggs into a bowl. Add the ground almonds, then the sugar, polenta, chopped almonds and cocoa powder. Using an electric mixer, beat at medium speed until combined. The mixture will be quite moist but not wet; you may need to add more ground almonds if it is too wet.

Press the mixture into the tin, cover with a sheet of baking parchment and press down firmly using the back of a spoon, making sure it is even and spread into the corners. Bake for 20–22 minutes, or until golden brown but still slightly soft. Leave in the tin to cool completely.

For the topping, melt 115 g/4 oz of the chocolate in a heatproof bowl set over a saucepan of gently simmering water, stirring until smooth (or in a microwave). Using a palette knife, spread this evenly over the base. Put into the fridge to set. Mix the olive oil with the lime zest and juice and stir well.

Crack the eggs into a mixing bowl. Add the ground almonds, then the sugar, polenta, mint leaves and peppermint oil. Pour in the olive oil and lime mixture. Using an electric mixer, beat at high speed until it forms a smooth batter. Spoon onto the base and spread evenly with a spatula. Bake for 30 minutes, until dark golden brown. Leave in the tin until completely cool.

Melt the remaining chocolate in a heatproof bowl set over a saucepan of gently simmering water, stirring until smooth (or in a microwave).

If making chocolate mint leaves, using a small, soft paintbrush, brush a little of this chocolate over 8 mint leaves. Place the leaves on a piece of baking parchment and put in the fridge for 30 minutes to set, then turn the leaves over and paint the other sides. Return to the fridge until completely set.

Drizzle the remaining chocolate over the cake using a metal spoon. If using, scatter the chocolate-coated leaves over the cake with some uncoated leaves.

Florentine slab

melted butter, for brushing
300 g/10½ oz dark chocolate, chopped
1 tbsp almond oil
200 g/7 oz condensed milk
115 g/4 oz natural colour glacé (candied) cherries, chopped
75 g/2¾ oz/generous ½ cup dried cranberries
50 g/1¾ oz/5 tbsp raisins
50 g/1¾ oz mixed (candied) peel
½ tsp salt
50 g/1¾ oz/⅓ cup almonds, toasted and roughly chopped
40 g/1½ oz/5 tbsp whole peanuts, toasted
25 g/1 oz/3 tbsp pistachios, toasted and roughly chopped
25 g/1 oz sunflower seeds, toasted

This is a quick-and-easy take on florentines. Just slide the whole florentine out of its baking tin onto a chunky wooden board and pop it in the centre of the table for guests to break bits off. Lovely when you fancy a little something sweet but can't face full-on pudding!

Cut a rectangle of baking parchment to line the bottom of a 30 x 23 x 4 cm/ 12 x 9 x 1½ in baking tin. Pop the parchment into the tin and brush it and the tin liberally with melted butter.

Melt the chocolate with the almond oil in a heatproof bowl set over a saucepan of gently simmering water, stirring until smooth (or in a microwave). Spread the melted chocolate evenly all over the bottom of the tin. Chill in the fridge for 1 hour, or until completely set.

Preheat the oven to 180°C/350°F/Gas 4. Put the condensed milk into a mixing bowl and add the glacé cherries, cranberries, raisins, mixed peel and salt. Mix together gently, using a wooden spoon, then add the toasted almonds, peanuts, pistachios and sunflower seeds and mix well.

Spread the mixture over the set chocolate. Bake for 15–17 minutes, until firm to the touch and golden brown. Leave to cool, then return to the fridge for 2 hours to reset the chocolate.

To serve, turn out onto a board and peel off the baking parchment before cutting it up – or let your friends break off their own pieces.

makes: 1 x 30 x 23 cm/ 12 x 9 in cake
health: gluten-free
cook: 15–17 minutes
store: 7 days in airtight container. Freezes well

For extra 'ooh-la-la'

Use a pastry cutter to cut into shapes and serve in pretty paper cases for an afternoon tea party.

Chocolate and orange truffle cake

makes: 1 x 30 x 23 cm/ 12 x 9 in cake
health: gluten-free
cook: 40–45 minutes
store: 7 days in airtight container
compost: eggshells, bits of orange

While cycling and camping in France we happened across a campsite with a very rustic eatery, complete with lean-to kitchen. We were given a fantastic meal, the most memorable component of which was the chocolate and orange cake, served in wafer-thin slices with a tiny espresso coffee.

- 150 g/5½ oz/scant ¾ cup butter, plus extra, melted, for brushing
- 600 g/1 lb 5 oz milk chocolate, cut into chunks
- 6 eggs
- 300 g/10½ oz/3 cups ground almonds
- 1 tbsp espresso coffee granules, dissolved in 1 tbsp hot water
- 1 tbsp orange oil

ROASTED ORANGE TOPPING

- ½ orange (sliced horizontally, in its skin)
- 3 tbsp light brown sugar
- 2 tbsp orange juice

CHOCOLATE-ORANGE TOPPING

- 50 g/1¾ oz dark chocolate, chopped
- 1 tbsp olive oil
- 1 tsp orange-blossom water

Preheat the oven to 180°C/350°F/Gas 4. Brush a 30 x 23 x 4 cm/12 x 9 x 1½ in baking tin liberally with melted butter.

To make the roasted orange topping, cut the orange half into 3–4 round slices and then cut each slice into quarters. Mix the sugar and orange juice together and spoon the mixture over the orange pieces. Roast for 15–20 minutes.

Melt the butter and milk chocolate in a heatproof bowl set over a saucepan of gently simmering water, stirring until smooth (or in a microwave).

Crack the eggs into a large mixing bowl. Add the almonds, coffee and orange oil, then add the melted chocolate-and-butter mixture. Using an electric mixer, beat at high speed until you have a smooth, pale brown mixture. It will thicken up as it cools.

Spoon the mixture into the tin and spread out evenly. Bang the tin firmly on a work surface to get rid of air pockets. Bake for 25 minutes, or until the surface springs back when pressed gently with your fingertips. A flat cake skewer will come out clean when the cake is ready. Leave to cool in the tin.

For the chocolate-orange topping, melt the dark chocolate with the olive oil and orange-blossom water in a heatproof bowl set over a saucepan of gently simmering water, stirring until smooth (or in a microwave). Spoon this mixture over the cake and smooth over with a palette knife. Allow the topping to set and then decorate with the roasted orange pieces.

For extra 'ooh-la-la'

Cut the traybake into small squares and sandwich pieces together with orange curd in the middle.

Rudolf's reward

makes: 12 cakes
health: gluten-free
store: 5 days in fridge. Freeze well

These chocolate rice crispy cakes are lovely for children to make – with grown-up help when melting the chocolate. They're so easy and fun to do. The process is messy but the results are very pretty, especially when you use metallic and patterned cake cases. As the name suggests, we originally introduced these as a Christmas special, but we nearly had a mutiny when we tried to take them off the menu.

125 g/4½ oz/generous ½ cup butter
125 g/4½ oz/6 tbsp golden syrup
85 g/3 oz milk chocolate, chopped
40 g/1½ oz dark chocolate, chopped
90 g/3¼ oz/generous 3 cups gluten-free rice crispies

TOPPING

50 g/1¾ oz milk chocolate buttons
20 g/¾ oz/1½ tbsp butter
20 g/¾ oz dark chocolate, chopped
12 whole natural colour glacé (candied) cherries

Put 12 pretty cake cases on a baking sheet.

Put the butter, golden syrup, milk chocolate and dark chocolate in a saucepan and melt over a medium-low heat, stirring until smooth (or in a microwave). The mixture should thicken slightly as you stir it, but if too hot will become runny. If this happens, stir well and set to one side to cool and thicken.

Weigh out the rice crispies into a large mixing bowl. Pour the melted mixture over the rice crispies and stir well with a wooden spoon until all of the rice crispies are well coated.

Using 2 metal dessertspoons, spoon the mixture into the 12 cake cases. Press the mixture gently into the case so that you have a reasonably solid little cake.

For the topping, sprinkle the milk chocolate buttons over the top of each cake, pushing them in slightly.

Melt the butter and dark chocolate in a heatproof bowl set over a saucepan of gently simmering water, stirring until smooth (or in a microwave). Pop a glacé cherry on each cake and drizzle the butter-and-chocolate mixture over the cakes with a metal spoon. Place in the fridge for 1 hour to set.

Baking tip

Make this in a shallow 30 x 23 x 4 cm/12 x 9 x 1½ in baking tin and, when set, cut into 15 pieces using a long sharp knife.

Double chocolate and raspberry tartlets

makes: 10 tartlets
health: gluten-free
cook: 18–20 minutes
store: best eaten on same day; overnight in fridge. Freeze well

melted butter, for brushing
tapioca flour, for dusting
300 g/10½ oz/3 cups pecan halves
60 g/2¼ oz/5 tbsp muscovado sugar
50 g/1¾ oz/4 tbsp butter, chilled and cubed
1 tsp salt

CHOCOLATE LINING

140 g/5 oz dark chocolate, chopped
2 tbsp almond oil

WHITE CHOCOLATE FILLING

225 ml/8 fl oz/scant 1 cup double (heavy) cream
100 ml/3½ fl oz/7 tbsp crème fraîche
100 g/3½ oz/7 tbsp Greek yogurt
1 tsp vanilla extract
175 g/6 oz white chocolate, chopped
2–3 g freeze-dried raspberries

DECORATION

350 g/12 oz/3 cups raspberries
1–2 tbsp icing (confectioners') sugar (optional)

The pastry for these tarts is easy to make, and after baking blind you can use the cases for all sorts of fillings. They won't tolerate any extra time in the oven, as the pecans become bitter. The robust flavour of the pastry lined with dark chocolate offsets the sweetness of the white chocolate.

Preheat the oven to 150°C/300°F/Gas 2. Brush 10 x 10 cm/4 in loose-bottomed tartlet tins with melted butter, then dust with tapioca flour. Place the tins on a large baking sheet. Cut out 10 discs of baking parchment to fit the tins; set aside.

Put the pecans, muscovado sugar, butter and salt into a food processor and whizz for 3–4 minutes, until the mixture forms a soft dough – chopped bits of pecan will be visible. The dough is sticky, so you may need to scrape the sides of the processor with a rubber spatula to get it all out. Squidge the mixture into the tartlet tins by hand, pressing it into the bottom and up the sides of the tins. Blind bake for 18–20 minutes; don't overbake or the pastry will crumble. Leave to cool.

For the chocolate lining, melt the dark chocolate with the almond oil in a heatproof bowl set over a saucepan of gently simmering water, stirring until smooth (or in a microwave). Pour the chocolate-and-almond mixture into the tartlet cases and spread with the back of a teaspoon to coat the bottom and sides of the tartlets in a thin layer. Keep any spare mixture to drizzle over the finished tartlets. Chill the tarts in the fridge for 30 minutes.

For the white chocolate filling, heat 100 ml/3½ fl oz/⅓ cup of the double cream with the crème fraiche, yogurt and vanilla in a saucepan until the mixture just boils. Remove from the heat and allow to cool slightly. Add the white chocolate and stir until it has melted. Chill the mixture in the fridge for 1 hour. Meanwhile, whizz the freeze-dried raspberries in a food processor. Whisk the remaining double cream until thick, then fold it into the cooled white chocolate mixture. Add the freeze-dried raspberries and stir. Spoon the mixture into the tartlets and chill them for 3 hours.

Decorate each tartlet with raspberries. Dredge icing sugar over them or drizzle with the spare chocolate lining mixture.

flapjacks

Hedgerow flapjacks

makes: 15 pieces
health: gluten-free
cook: 33–38 minutes
store: 5 days in airtight container. Freeze well

185 g/6½ oz/generous ¾ cup butter, plus extra, melted, for brushing
115 g/4 oz/generous ½ cup light brown sugar
125 g/4½ oz/6 tbsp golden syrup
225 g/8 oz/2¾ cups gluten-free oats
100 g/3½ oz gluten-free oat flour
200 g/7 oz/1½ cups hazelnuts, toasted and half of them chopped
50 g/1¾ oz/⅔ cup hazelnuts, ground
about 350 g/12 oz/3 cups blackcurrants or other seasonal soft fruit, or 200 g/7 oz blackcurrant curd or jam

CRUMBLE TOPPING

100 g/3½ oz/½ cup light brown sugar
100 g/3½ oz/scant ½ cup butter, chilled and cubed
55 g/2 oz/scant ¾ cup gluten-free oats
50 g/1¾ oz gluten-free oat flour
50 g/1¾ oz sorghum flour

The Dorset hedgerows are very generous in late summer and early autumn. They provide wild raspberries, blackberries, hazelnuts, damsons and much more. Do feel free to use any hedgerow or soft fruit, depending on the season: try redcurrants, blackcurrants (which I much prefer to blueberries) or even the teensy, intensely sweet wild strawberries. Or try Alpine strawberries, which we grow in hanging baskets.

Preheat the oven to 180°C/350°F/Gas 4. Cut a rectangle of baking parchment to line the bottom of a 30 x 23 x 4 cm/12 x 9 x 1½ in baking tin. Pop the parchment into the tin and brush it and the tin liberally with melted butter.

Put the butter, sugar and syrup into a saucepan and melt over a low heat, stirring every minute or so with a wooden spoon. Cook for 8–10 minutes until all the sugar has dissolved (when the bottom of the pan no longer feels gritty, the mixture is ready). Don't let the mixture boil or the flapjacks will be hard.

Put the oats, oat flour and whole, chopped and ground hazelnuts into a large mixing bowl and stir. Pour in the melted butter mixture and stir well, using a rubber spatula. Ensure that all the dry ingredients are well coated.

Spoon the mixture into the tin and spread evenly, using a rubber spatula – you need to push it into the corners and create a fairly smooth surface. Scatter over enough fresh fruit to cover. Alternatively, spread a thick layer of blackcurrant curd or jam over the base. Bake for 10 minutes.

To make the crumble topping, put the sugar, butter, oats, oat flour and sorghum flour into a large mixing bowl and rub the butter into the dry ingredients using your fingertips. It will soon become clumpy – it is very soft and buttery, wetter than a typical crumble topping.

Use your fingers to scatter the crumble topping over the fruit. You don't need to be too fussy about covering the fruit completely. Press the crumble mix down quite firmly. Bake for 15–18 minutes, until light golden. Leave to cool, or serve warm with top-quality vanilla ice cream.

Spiced pear and raisin flapjacks

makes: 15 pieces
health: gluten-free
cook: 48–54 minutes
store: 5 days in fridge. Freeze well
compost: pear trimmings

185 g/6½ oz/generous ¾ cup butter, plus extra, melted, for brushing
100 g/3½ oz/½ cup light brown sugar
60 g/2¼ oz/3 tbsp golden syrup
70 g/2½ oz/3½ tbsp clear honey
pinch of salt
250 g/9 oz/3 cups gluten-free oats
150 g/5½ oz/generous 1½ cups ground almonds
50 g/1¾ oz gluten-free oat flour
100 g/3½ oz/generous ½ cup raisins
1½ tsp mixed spice
½ tsp ground ginger

ROASTED PEARS

350 g/12 oz pears (2–3 pears)
1 tsp mixed spice
3 tbsp clear honey

This is a lovely recipe for when pears are in season. Any type of pear works well here.

Preheat the oven to 180°C/350°F/Gas 4. Cut a rectangle of baking parchment to line the bottom of a 30 x 23 x 4 cm/12 x 9 x 1½ in baking tin. Pop in the parchment and brush it and the tin liberally with melted butter.

For the roasted pears, core the pears (keep the skin on) and cut into roughly 1 cm/½ in cubes. Place in a roasting tin, sprinkle with the mixed spice and drizzle with the honey. Bake for 20–22 minutes, until soft. Weigh them: you should have about 280 g/10 oz. Keep the liquid to use in the flapjack.

Put the butter, sugar, syrup, honey and salt into a saucepan and melt over a low heat, stirring every minute or so with a wooden spoon. Cook for 8–10 minutes, until all the sugar has dissolved (when the bottom of the pan no longer feels gritty, the mixture is ready). Don't let the mixture boil or the flapjacks will be hard.

Put the oats, almonds, oat flour, raisins, mixed spice and ground ginger into a large mixing bowl and stir. Pour in the melted butter mixture and stir well using a rubber spatula. Ensure that all the dry ingredients are well coated. Gently stir in 150 g/5½ oz of the roasted pears, along with the liquid from all the roasted pears, taking care to keep the pear cubes intact.

Spoon the mixture into the tin and spread evenly, using a rubber spatula – you need to push it into the corners and create a fairly smooth surface. Bake for 20–22 minutes, until golden.

While still warm and soft, press the remaining roasted pear pieces into the top of the flapjack. Leave to cool and set – up to 3 hours. This is a very moist flapjack, so needs careful handling.

For extra 'ooh-la-la'

Once cooled, cut the flapjack into pieces and half-dip them in melted dark chocolate.

Honeybuns
gorgeous cakes

Date and orange flapjacks

almond oil or vegetable oil, for brushing
300 g/10½ oz/1½ cups light brown sugar
300 g/10½ oz/1¼ cups dairy-free spread
175 g/6 oz/½ cup golden syrup
125 g/4½ oz/6 tbsp clear honey
600 g/1 lb 5 oz/7¼ cups gluten-free oats
125 g/4½ oz chestnut flour

FILLING

100 g/3½ oz/¾ cup pitted dates
200 g/7 oz/generous ½ cup good-quality orange marmalade
finely grated zest of 1 orange

TOPPING

2 tbsp good-quality orange marmalade

These beauties are dairy-free as well as gluten-free. They're best baked in bendy silicone bun cases. The marmalade really does need to be good, and its citrus bite helps balance the sweetness of the dates.

Preheat the oven to 180°C/350°F/Gas 4. Brush 24 x bendy silicone bun cases (or 2 x 12-cup bendy silicone muffin pans) with almond oil and place on a baking sheet.

Put the sugar, dairy-free spread, syrup and honey into a saucepan and melt over a low heat, stirring every minute or so with a wooden spoon. Cook for 8–10 minutes, until all the sugar has dissolved (when the bottom of the pan no longer feels gritty, the mixture is ready). Don't let the mixture boil or the flapjacks will be hard.

Put the oats and chestnut flour into a large mixing bowl and stir. Pour in the sugar-and-syrup mixture and stir well, using a rubber spatula. Ensure that all the dry ingredients are well coated.

For the filling, chop the dates roughly into thirds and mix them in a bowl with the marmalade and orange zest.

Spoon the flapjack mixture into the bun cases using 2 metal tablespoons. Half-fill each case, add a teaspoon of the filling, then fill to the top with more flapjack mixture. Bake for 15 minutes, until golden.

For the topping, gently heat the marmalade and brush over the flapjacks while they're still warm. Allow to cool completely before turning out.

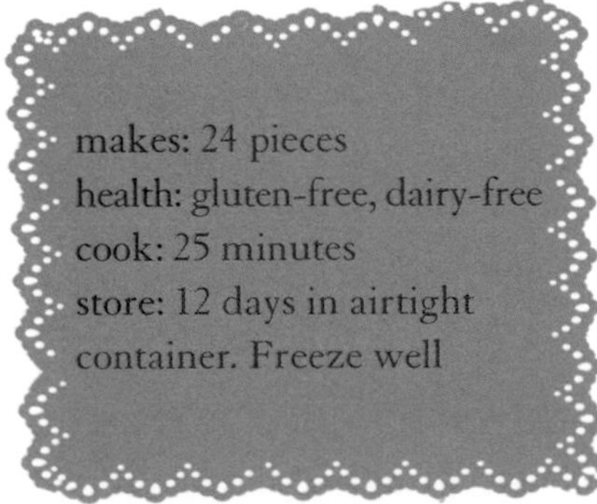

For extra 'ooh-la-la'

For special occasions, top with a pitted Medjool date.

Apricot butterjacks

makes: 12
health: gluten-free
cook: 20–25 minutes
store: 7 days in airtight container. Freeze well

185 g/6½ oz/generous ¾ cup butter, plus extra, melted, for brushing
125 g/4½ oz/generous ½ cup light brown sugar
50 g/1¾ oz/2½ tbsp golden syrup
50 g/1¾ oz/2½ tbsp clear honey
½ tsp salt
300 g/10½ oz/3½ cups gluten-free oats
60 g/2¼ oz/½ cup dried apricots, chopped
25 g/1 oz/5 tbsp coconut chips
25 g/1 oz coconut flour
½ tsp vanilla extract

TOPPING

6 soft dried apricots
3 tbsp apricot jam

When we moved to Dorset we were thrilled with the quality of the local butter and wanted to create a product to celebrate and showcase it. There's something about these buttery treats that gets you hooked.

Preheat the oven to 180°C/350°F/Gas 4. Brush a 12-cup bendy silicone muffin pan with melted butter and place on a metal baking sheet.

Put the butter, sugar, syrup, honey and salt into a saucepan and melt over a low heat, stirring every minute or so with a wooden spoon. Cook for 8–10 minutes, until all the sugar has dissolved (when the bottom of the pan no longer feels gritty, the mixture is ready). Don't let the mixture boil or the flapjacks will be hard.

Put the oats, dried apricots, coconut chips, coconut flour and vanilla into a large mixing bowl and stir. Pour in the melted butter mixture and stir well, using a rubber spatula. Ensure that all the dry ingredients are well coated.

Spoon the mixture into the bun cases using 2 metal tablespoons. Fill the bun cases right to the top and don't smooth them over – these are meant to look rustic! Press a dried apricot onto 6 of the buns. Bake for 12–15 minutes, until golden brown. While still warm from the oven, press your thumb into the top of the 6 buns without an apricot and spoon in ½ tsp apricot jam. Gently heat the remaining 1 tbsp apricot jam until it melts slightly, then brush over the apricot-topped buns. Leave to cool completely.

Baking tip

Don't use paper cases as the butter will seep through. You could make this in a shallow 30 x 23 x 4 cm/12 x 9 x 1½ in baking tin lined with baking parchment; increase the baking time by about 5 minutes.

Fig and almond flapjacks

185 g/6½ oz/generous ¾ cup butter, plus extra, melted, for brushing
115 g/4 oz/generous ½ cup light brown sugar
70 g/2½ oz/3½ tbsp clear honey
60 g/2¼ oz/3 tbsp golden syrup
½ tsp salt
200 g/7 oz/2 cups ground almonds
200 g/7 oz/2⅓ cups gluten-free oats
100 g/3½ oz gluten-free oat flour
100 g/3½ oz/¾ cup almonds, toasted and chopped
85 g/3 oz/3 cups gluten-free cornflakes
75g/2¾ oz/½ cup dried figs, chopped
⅓ tsp orange oil

TOPPING

3 dried figs, quartered
2 tbsp clear honey

On a trip to Portugal as a student I was bowled over by 3 things in particular: the fresh sardines, grilled while we watched; the market where we bought dried figs studded with whole almonds – a perfect snack for my friend Pat and me as we cycled along the Algarve coastline. The third? Medronho, the local firewater. Very messy.

Preheat the oven to 180°C/350°F/Gas 4. Brush a 12-cup bendy silicone muffin pan with melted butter and place on a metal baking sheet.

Put the butter, sugar, honey, syrup and salt into a saucepan and melt over a low heat, stirring every minute or so with a wooden spoon. Cook for 8–10 minutes, until all the sugar has dissolved (when the bottom of the pan no longer feels gritty, the mixture is ready). Don't let the mixture boil or the flapjacks will be hard.

Put the ground almonds, oats, oat flour, chopped almonds, cornflakes, chopped figs and orange oil into a large mixing bowl and stir. Pour in the melted butter mixture and stir well, using a rubber spatula. Ensure that all the dry ingredients are well coated.

Spoon the mixture into the muffin cups. Make an indentation on top of each flapjack. Bake for 12–15 minutes, until golden brown. While still warm, place a piece of dried fig on top of each flapjack, pressing in slightly, and then drizzle with honey.

makes: 12 pieces
health: gluten-free
cook: 20–25 minutes
store: 10 days in airtight container. Freeze well

Make it dairy-free

For a dairy-free version of this flapjack, replace the butter with dairy-free spread.

Granola bars

makes: 15 pieces
health: gluten-free, dairy-free
cook: 23–27 minutes
store: 10 days in airtight container. Freeze well

100 ml/3½ fl oz/⅓ cup almond oil, plus extra for brushing
200 g/7 oz/1 cup light brown sugar
3 tbsp clear honey
100 g/3½ oz/¾ cup hazelnuts, chopped
100 g/3½ oz/1 cup walnuts, chopped
40 g/1½ oz/scant ½ cup ground almonds

COCONUT, NUTS AND SEEDS FOR TOASTING
50 g/1¾ oz/generous ½ cup coconut chips
50 g/1¾ oz// tbsp pistachios, chopped
40 g/1½ oz/4½ tbsp pine nuts
25 g/1 oz/3 tbsp sesame seeds
25 g/1 oz sunflower seeds

This is a nutritious afternoon snack or a quick breakfast on the run, packed with the goodness of nuts and seeds.

Preheat the oven to 180°C/350°F/Gas 4. Cut a rectangle of baking parchment to line the bottom of a 30 x 23 x 4 cm/12 x 9 x 1½ in baking tin. Pop the parchment in the tin and brush it and the tin liberally with almond oil.

Place the coconut, nuts and seeds for toasting on a baking sheet and spread them thinly. Toast in the oven for 5 minutes, then allow to cool.

Put the almond oil, sugar and honey into a saucepan and melt over a medium heat, stirring every minute or so with a wooden spoon. Cook for 8–10 minutes, until all the sugar has dissolved (when the bottom of the pan no longer feels gritty, the mixture is ready). Bring to the boil and allow to simmer for a minute or 2, stirring all the time until the mixture begins to caramelize. The almond oil will sit on top and not mix in.

Put the hazelnuts, walnuts and ground almonds into a large mixing bowl, add the toasted coconut, nuts and seeds and stir. Pour in the melted sugar mixture and stir well using a rubber spatula. Ensure that all the dry ingredients are well coated.

Spoon the mixture into the tin and spread evenly, using the rubber spatula – you need to push it into the corners and create a fairly smooth surface. Bake for 10–12 minutes, until golden. Allow to cool and set completely (this can take up to 4 hours) before removing from the tin and cutting into bars.

Give it a twist

For a breakfast granola, crumble the bars and serve with plain yogurt and fresh fruit.

Cranberry, pecan and maple syrup flapjacks

185 g/6½ oz/generous ¾ cup butter, plus extra, melted, for brushing
115 g/4 oz/generous ½ cup light brown sugar
70 g/2½ oz/3½ tbsp golden syrup
3 tbsp maple syrup
½ tsp salt
150 g/5½ oz/generous 1¾ cups gluten-free oats
100 g/3½ oz gluten-free oat flour
100 g/3½ oz/1 cup pecan halves, toasted
50 g/1¾ oz/½ cup pecan halves, toasted and chopped
85 g/3 oz millet flakes
70 g/2½ oz/generous ½ cup dried cranberries
finely grated zest of 1 orange
½ tsp orange oil

TOPPING

25 g/1 oz/3 tbsp dried cranberries
finely grated zest of 1 orange
3 tbsp maple syrup

makes: 15 pieces
health: gluten-free
cook: 23–27 minutes
store: 2 weeks in airtight container. Freeze well

These are generously laden with pecans, and the maple syrup marries really well with both the pecans and the cranberries. It really is worth going to the effort of toasting the pecans.

Preheat the oven to 170°C/325°F/Gas 3. Cut a rectangle of baking parchment to line the bottom of a 30 x 23 x 4 cm/12 x 9 x 1½ in baking tin. Pop the parchment in the tin and brush it and the tin liberally with melted butter.

Put the butter, sugar, golden syrup, maple syrup and salt into a saucepan and melt over a low heat, stirring every minute or so with a wooden spoon. Cook for 8–10 minutes, until all the sugar has dissolved (when the bottom of the pan no longer feels gritty, the mixture is ready). Don't let the mixture boil or the flapjacks will be hard.

Put the oats, oat flour, halved and chopped pecans, millet flakes, dried cranberries, orange zest and orange oil into a large mixing bowl and stir. Pour in the melted butter mixture and stir well, using a rubber spatula. Ensure that all the dry ingredients are well coated.

Spoon the mixture into the tin and spread evenly, using a rubber spatula – you need to push it into the corners, but leave the surface fairly lumpy for a rustic effect. For the topping, scatter the cranberries over the surface, pressing them in lightly.

Bake for 15–17 minutes, until golden with slightly darker edges. It will be bubbling and quite soft when you take it from the oven, but will firm up as it cools. Leave in the tin to cool for 10 minutes, then transfer to a rack.

Mix the grated orange zest with the maple syrup and drizzle it over the flapjack while it is still warm. Cut up into 15 slices.

Make the most of your freezer

The uncooked mixture can be chilled in the fridge or frozen and then baked later – add another 5–10 minutes to cook from frozen.

Honey and almond sunshine slices

makes: 15 pieces
health: gluten-free, dairy-free
cook: 24–28 minutes
store: 7 days in airtight container. Freeze well

almond oil, for brushing
185 g/6½ oz/generous ¾ cup dairy-free spread
115 g/4 oz/generous ½ cup light brown sugar
100 g/3½ oz/5 tbsp clear honey
25 g/1 oz/1 tbsp golden syrup
200 g/7 oz/7 cups gluten-free cornflakes, lightly crushed
150 g/5½ oz/generous 1½ cups ground almonds
100 g/3½ oz/¾ cup almonds, toasted and chopped
25 g/1 oz millet flakes
pinch of salt

TOPPING

25 g/1 oz sunflower seeds

Dairy-free as well as gluten-free, these are really versatile snacks, perfect for breakfast or brunch on the run or for teatime. Farmers' markets are a great place to source good-quality local honey.

Preheat the oven to 170°C/325°F/Gas 3. Cut a rectangle of baking parchment to line the bottom of a 30 x 23 x 4 cm/12 x 9 x 1½ in baking tin. Pop the parchment into the tin and brush it and the tin liberally with almond oil.

Put the dairy-free spread, sugar, honey and syrup into a saucepan and melt over a low heat, stirring every minute or so with a wooden spoon. Cook for 8–10 minutes, until all the sugar has dissolved (when the bottom of the pan no longer feels gritty, the mixture is ready). Don't let the mixture boil or the flapjack will be hard. Leave to cool for 30 minutes.

Put the cornflakes, ground and chopped almonds, millet flakes and salt into a large mixing bowl and stir. Pour in the honey mixture and stir well, using a rubber spatula. Ensure that all the dry ingredients are well coated.

Spoon the mixture into the tin and spread evenly, using the rubber spatula – you need to push it into the corners and press down very firmly. Sprinkle the sunflower seeds over the top.

Bake for 16–18 minutes, until golden. Leave in the tin to cool, then cut into 15 slices.

Give it a twist

Substitute your own favourite gluten-free cereal for the cornflakes.

Treacle and chocolate flapjacks

250 g/9 oz/generous 1 cup butter, plus extra, melted, for brushing
150 g/5½ oz/¾ cup muscovado sugar
150 g/5½ oz/7 tbsp black treacle (molasses)
300 g/10½ oz millet flakes
125 g/4½ oz quinoa flour
60 g/2¼ oz/⅔ cup ground almonds

TOPPING

250 g/9 oz dark chocolate, chopped
2 tbsp black treacle (molasses)
1 tbsp almond oil

These oat-free flapjacks celebrate the intense, bittersweet flavour of black treacle (molasses). Admittedly it's a food people either love or hate, but if you are a fan, then we're quietly confident that you'll find this dangerously moreish. If you need more convincing to give it a whirl, black treacle is an excellent source of iron, calcium and B vitamins. Once cooled, this is easy to cut and is ideal for autumn picnics or packed lunches.

Preheat the oven to 180°C/350°F/Gas 4. Cut a rectangle of baking parchment to line the bottom of a 30 x 23 x 4 cm/12 x 9 x 1½ in baking tin. Pop the parchment into the tin and brush it and the tin liberally with melted butter.

Put the butter, sugar and treacle into a saucepan and melt over a low heat, stirring every minute or so with a wooden spoon. Cook for 8–10 minutes, until all the sugar has dissolved (when the bottom of the pan no longer feels gritty, the mixture is ready). Don't let the mixture boil or the flapjacks will be hard.

Put the millet, quinoa flour and almonds into a large mixing bowl and stir. Pour in the melted butter mixture and stir well, using a rubber spatula. Ensure that all the dry ingredients are well coated.

Spoon the mixture into the tin and spread evenly, using the rubber spatula – you need to push it into the corners and press down very firmly to make a thin layer. Bake for 14 minutes, until mid-golden. Leave in the tin to cool slightly.

To make the topping, melt the chocolate with the treacle and almond oil in a heatproof bowl set over a saucepan of gently simmering water, stirring until smooth (or in a microwave). Spread this mixture over the base. Leave to cool for about 14 minutes, then place in the fridge to set. Cut into 15 slices.

makes: 15 pieces
health: gluten-free
cook: 22–24 minutes
store: 12 days in airtight container. Freeze well

For extra 'ooh-la-la'

Add 1 tbsp cocoa powder to the base mixture – chocolate and treacle are natural bedfellows.

cookies and biscuits

Bourbon creams

makes: 12 biscuits
health: gluten-free
cook: 15–17 minutes
store: 5 days in airtight container. Cookies and dough freeze well
compost: eggshells

150 g/5½ oz/¾ cup light brown sugar
150 g/5½ oz/1¼ cups polenta
150 g/5½ oz/generous 1½ cups ground almonds
100 ml/3½ fl oz olive oil
2 eggs
50 g/1¾ oz/5 tbsp ground brown flax seeds (linseed)
20 g/¾ oz/2 tbsp brown rice flour
2 tbsp cocoa powder
1 tsp vanilla extract
tapioca flour, for dusting

CHOCOLATE CREAM FILLING

200 ml/7 fl oz double (heavy) cream
175 g/6 oz dark chocolate, chopped
4 tbsp icing (confectioners') sugar
1 tbsp cocoa powder

CHOCOLATE TOPPING

50 g/1¾ oz dark chocolate, chopped
50 g/1¾ oz milk chocolate, chopped

I remember my misspent student days very fondly … philosophising with Pat and Beks over a huge pot of tea and at least 1 packet of bourbons or custard creams. Hopefully we've captured some of the bourbon magic in this recipe, for those partial to a bit of tea, sympathy and biscuit nostalgia.

Preheat the oven to 180°C/350°F/Gas 4. Cut pieces of baking parchment to line the bottom of 2 large baking sheets.

Put the sugar, polenta, almonds, olive oil, eggs, flax seeds, rice flour, cocoa and vanilla into a large mixing bowl and beat using an electric mixer at low speed until the mixture forms a soft dough.

Dust your hands, rolling pin and work surface lightly with tapioca flour. Knead the dough gently and then roll it out to about 5 mm/¼ in thick. Using a 6 cm/2½ in heart-shaped pastry cutter, cut out biscuits and place them on the baking sheet, spacing them well apart. Bake for 12–14 minutes, until mid-brown and firm to the touch (they get firmer as they cool). Leave on the baking sheet for 5–10 minutes, then transfer to a rack to cool completely.

For the chocolate filling, heat the cream in a saucepan until just below boiling point. Remove from the heat and add the chocolate, whisking as you go. The mixture will thicken. Sift in the icing sugar, followed by the cocoa, and stir. Chill in the fridge for 30 minutes, or until thick enough to put into a piping bag.

Turn half of the biscuits upside-down and pipe the cream in swirls on top. Cover with the remaining biscuits – with the nice side facing upwards.

For the chocolate topping, melt the dark chocolate and milk chocolate together in a heatproof bowl set over a saucepan of gently simmering water, stirring until smooth (or in a microwave). Spoon about 1 tsp of melted chocolate onto each heart, smoothing it over with the back of the spoon.

Make the most of your freezer

Make and bake the cookies, freeze, then thaw them and pipe on the filling at your leisure.

Triple chocolate tinkers

makes: 12 cookies
health: gluten-free
cook: 15 minutes
store: 7 days in airtight container. Freeze well
compost: eggshell

150 g/5½ oz gluten-free oat flour
125 g/4½ oz/generous ½ cup butter, chilled and cubed
115g/4 oz/generous ½ cup granulated sugar
115g/4 oz/scant 1½ cups gluten-free oats
1 egg
1 tsp gluten-free baking powder
1 tsp vanilla extract
100 g/3½ oz dark chocolate, chopped
100 g/3½ oz milk chocolate, chopped
100 g/3½ oz white chocolate, chopped
tapioca flour, for dusting

TOPPING
115g/4 oz dark chocolate, chopped
55 g/2 oz/4 tbsp butter

These chocolatey cookies have achieved cult status among our loyal fans and customers.

Preheat the oven to 180°C/350°F/Gas 4. Cut a piece of baking parchment to line the bottom of a large baking sheet.

Put the oat flour, butter, sugar, oats, egg, baking powder and vanilla into a bowl and beat using an electric mixer at low speed until they start to clump together. Using a rubber spatula, stir in the dark, milk and white chocolate pieces.

Dust your hands and work surface liberally with tapioca flour. Knead the dough gently and then divide it into 12 equal portions. Roll into balls and place on the baking sheet. The cookies will spread as they bake, so make sure you leave plenty of space between them. Using the palms of your hands, squash each cookie into a disc about 1 cm/½ in thick.

Bake for 15 minutes, until light golden on top and mid-golden underneath: use a fish slice to check the bottom of a cookie after 13 minutes. Leave on the baking sheet for 5–10 minutes, then transfer to a rack.

For the topping, melt the chocolate and butter in a heatproof bowl set over a saucepan of gently simmering water, stirring until smooth (or in a microwave). Using a spoon, drizzle the mixture over the cookies.

Give it a twist

Instead of drizzling the chocolate and butter mixture over the cookies, you could half-dip them in it.

Scrumdiddleyumptious cookies

70 g/2½ oz stem ginger in syrup (drained weight), plus 2 tbsp drained, chopped stem ginger for topping
4 egg whites
400 g/14 oz/2 cups vanilla sugar
200 g/7 oz/2 cups ground almonds
200 g/7 oz/scant 3 cups hazelnuts, ground
1 tsp lemon oil
2 tsp lemon curd
finely grated zest of 2 unwaxed lemons
4 tbsp icing (confectioners') sugar, plus extra for dusting

This is a variation on our Amondi cookies (see page 130). The lemon and ginger both cut through the sweetness in just the right way. We enjoy ours with a cup of lemongrass tea.

Preheat the oven to 180°C/350°F/Gas 4. Cut a piece of baking parchment to line the bottom of a large baking sheet. Crush the 70 g/2½ oz stem ginger in a food processor or blender.

Put the egg whites into a large mixing bowl and whisk with an electric mixer until they form stiff peaks. Add the sugar, almonds, hazelnuts, lemon oil, lemon curd and lemon zest and beat using an electric mixer at low speed until you have quite a wet dough.

Dust your hands with icing sugar and divide the dough into 14 equal portions. Roll into balls and roll these in the icing sugar, then place on the baking sheet. The cookies will spread as they bake, so make sure you leave plenty of space between them. Using the palms of your hands, squash each cookie to a disc about 1 cm/½ in thick.

Using your fingertip, make a small hollow in the top of each cookie and pop about ⅓ tsp chopped stem ginger into it.

Bake for 14–16 minutes, until light golden on top and mid-golden underneath: use a fish slice to check the bottom of a cookie after 14 minutes. Leave on the baking sheet for 5–10 minutes, then transfer to a rack.

makes: 14 cookies
health: gluten-free
cook: 14–16 minutes
store: 7 days in airtight container. Freeze well
compost: eggshells

For crumbs to coat desserts

To make Scrumdiddleyumptious crumbs for decorating desserts, cook the cookies for 25–30 minutes, until dark golden brown and firm. Leave to cool and then crumble in a food processor. Store in an airtight container in the freezer.

Amondi cookies

makes: 14 cookies
health: gluten-free, dairy-free
cook: 15–18 minutes
store: 7 days in airtight container. Freeze well
compost: eggshell

This is our version of Italian amaretti. While writing this book we've fallen in love with a few more naturally gluten-free ingredients such as flax seeds (linseed) and sorghum flour. Both work really well with ground almonds – they add lightness and help to balance the oiliness of the nuts – so we've adapted our usual Amondi to include ground flax seeds.

- 4 egg whites
- 400 g/14 oz/4 cups ground almonds
- 280 g/10 oz/generous 1¼ cups granulated sugar
- 50 g/1¾ oz/5 tbsp ground brown flax seeds (linseed)
- 1 tsp orange oil
- finely grated zest of 2 oranges
- 4 tbsp icing (confectioners') sugar
- 14 whole almonds

Preheat the oven to 180°C/350°F/Gas 4. Cut a piece of baking parchment to line the bottom of a large baking sheet.

Put the egg whites into a large clean mixing bowl and whisk with an electric mixer until they form stiff peaks. Add the ground almonds, sugar, flax seeds, orange oil and orange zest and beat using an electric mixer at low speed until you have a sticky dough.

Dust your hands with icing sugar and divide the dough into 14 equal portions. Roll into balls and roll these in the icing sugar, then place on the baking sheet. The cookies will spread as they bake, so make sure you leave plenty of space between them. Using the palms of your hands, squash each cookie to a disc about 1 cm/½ in thick. Place a whole almond in the centre of each cookie and push it in gently.

Bake for 15–18 minutes, until light golden on top and mid-golden underneath: use a fish slice to check the bottom of a cookie after 15 minutes. Leave on the baking sheet for 5–10 minutes, then transfer to a cooling rack. When cold, Amondi should be firm and chewy, but not hard.

Make the most of your freezer

Make double the amount and freeze. Amondi cookies are used in other recipes: Chockabloc (page 95) and Bumble Barrow fruit cake (page 20).

Spicy cat cookies

makes: 12 cookies
health: gluten-free
cook: 15–17 minutes
store: 5 days in airtight container. Cookies and dough freeze well
compost: eggshell

115g/4 oz stem ginger in syrup (drained weight)
1 egg
150 g/5½ oz/generous ¾ cup ground brown flax seeds (linseed)
125 g/4½ oz/generous ½ cup butter, chilled and grated
115g/4 oz/generous ½ cup granulated sugar
100 g/3½ oz/generous ½ cup plump raisins
115g/4 oz/scant 1½ cups gluten-free oats
40 g/1½ oz gluten-free oat flour
1 tsp gluten-free baking powder
1 tsp vanilla extract
tapioca flour, for dusting

If you like ginger, you'll love these raisin and ginger cookies.

Preheat the oven to 180°C/350°F/Gas 4. Cut a piece of baking parchment to line the bottom of a large baking sheet. Crush the stem ginger in a food processor.

Put all of the ingredients (except the tapioca flour) into a bowl and beat using an electric mixer at low speed until they start to clump together. The dough may be quite sticky, as the ginger is moist.

Dust your hands and work surface liberally with tapioca flour. Knead the dough gently and then divide it into 12 equal portions. Roll into balls and place on the baking sheet. The cookies will spread as they bake, so make sure you leave plenty of space between them. Using the palms of your hands, squash each cookie to a disc about 1 cm/½ in thick.

Bake for 15–17 minutes, until light golden on top and mid-golden underneath: use a fish slice to check the bottom of a cookie after 15 minutes. Leave on the baking sheet for 5–10 minutes, then transfer to a rack.

Give it a twist

Try making these as mini cookies – about 3 cm/1 in each – (reduce the baking time by about 5 minutes) and sandwich together with mascarpone mixed with chopped stem ginger.

Peanut butter and chocolate cookies

1 egg
150 g/5½ oz chestnut flour
125 g/4½ oz/generous ½ cup butter, chilled and grated
115g/4 oz/generous ½ cup granulated sugar
115g/4 oz crunchy peanut butter
115g/4 oz/scant 1½ cups gluten-free oats
1 tsp gluten-free baking powder
1 tsp vanilla extract
¼ tsp salt
150 g/5½ oz milk chocolate, cut into chunks
tapioca flour, for dusting

These cookies are easy to make and devilishly moreish. They're also great made as smaller cookies and sandwiched together with peanut butter mixed with melted chocolate.

Preheat the oven to 180°C/350°F/Gas 4. Cut a piece of baking parchment to line the bottom of a large baking sheet.

Put the egg, chestnut flour, butter, sugar, peanut butter, oats, baking powder, vanilla and salt into a bowl and beat using an electric mixer at low speed until they start to clump together. Using a rubber spatula, stir in the chocolate chunks.

Dust your hands and work surface liberally with tapioca flour. Knead the dough gently and then divide it into 12 equal portions. Roll into balls and place on the baking sheet. The cookies will spread as they bake, so make sure you leave plenty of space between them. Using the palms of your hands, squash each cookie into a disc about 1 cm/½ in thick.

Bake for 12–15 minutes, until light golden on top and mid-golden underneath: use a fish slice to check the bottom of a cookie after 12 minutes. Leave on the baking sheet for 5–10 minutes, then transfer to a rack.

makes: 12
health: gluten-free
cook: 12–15 minutes
store: 5 days in airtight container. Freeze well
compost: eggshell

For extra 'ooh-la-la'

To take them to the next level, cover with melted milk chocolate.

Pistachio pitstops

100 g/3½ oz/generous ¾ cup pistachios, toasted
20 g/¾ oz/1½ tbsp light brown sugar
½ tsp salt
3–4 tsp clear honey

TOPPING

2 freeze-dried raspberries

These little mouthfuls remind me of lazy days on holiday in Greece. They're so simple to make and lovely to share with friends over a glass of lemonade or cup of coffee in the garden. They are dairy-free as well as gluten-free.

Preheat the oven to 180°C/350°F/Gas 4. Cut a piece of baking parchment to line the bottom of a large baking sheet.

Once the toasted pistachios are cold, put them in a food processor with the sugar, salt and 3 tsp of honey and blitz to fine crumbs. The mixture should clump together, so you may need to add another 1 tsp of honey – it depends on the oil content of the pistachios. (It should not be left standing for too long, otherwise the honey will be absorbed by the nuts and the dough will become too crumbly to handle.)

Divide the dough into about 20 equal portions. Roll into balls and place on the baking sheet. The biscuits will spread as they bake, so make sure you leave plenty of space between them. Using the palms of your hands, squash each ball into a disc about 5 mm/¼ in thick. Bake for 5–6 minutes, until golden.

For the topping, crush the freeze-dried raspberries with a fork. While the cookies are still warm, sprinkle the crumbs on top of each cookie, pressing them on gently. Best eaten while still warm.

makes: 20 mini cookies
health: gluten-free, dairy-free
cook: 5–6 minutes
store: 5 days in airtight container (without raspberry topping). Freeze well

For extra 'ooh-la-la'

Once cooled, half-dip in melted dairy-free dark chocolate.

Custard creams

makes: 16 biscuits
health: gluten-free
cook: 12–14 minutes
store: 7 days in airtight container. Freeze well
compost: eggshell

150 g/5½ oz/generous ½ cup butter, softened and cubed
150 g/5½ oz/¾ cup caster (superfine) sugar
150 g/5½ oz/1¼ cups polenta
150 g/5½ oz/generous 1½ cups ground almonds
100 g/3½ oz custard powder
1 egg
½ tsp vanilla extract
tapioca flour, for dusting

FILLING

250 g/9 oz/generous 1 cup butter, softened
100 g/3½ oz/¾ cup icing (confectioners') sugar
2 tbsp custard powder
½ tsp vanilla extract

TO DECORATE

1–2 tbsp icing (confectioners') sugar, sifted

We do love the classic British custard creams; here, we've reinterpreted them in fabulous gluten-free form.

Preheat the oven to 170°C/325°F/Gas 3. Cut pieces of baking parchment to line the bottom of 2 large baking sheets.

Put the butter, sugar, polenta, almonds, custard powder, egg and vanilla into a large mixing bowl and beat using an electric mixer at low speed until the mixture forms a soft dough.

Dust your hands, rolling pin and work surface lightly with tapioca flour. Knead the dough gently and then roll out to about 5 mm/¼ in thick. Using a pastry cutter (we used a 6 cm/2½ in heart-shaped cutter), cut out the dough and place the shapes on the baking sheets. The biscuits will spread as they bake, so make sure you leave plenty of space between them.

Bake for 12–14 minutes, until golden and firm to the touch (they get firmer as they cool). Leave on the baking sheets for 5–10 minutes, then transfer to a rack.

To make the filling, put the butter into a mixing bowl. Sift the icing sugar and custard powder into the bowl, add the vanilla and beat using an electric mixer at medium speed until smooth. Chill in the fridge for 30 minutes.

Spoon the filling into a piping bag fitted with a small star nozzle. Turn half of the biscuits upside down and pipe the cream in swirls on top. Cover with the remaining biscuits – with the nice side facing upwards.

To decorate, place a paper doily over the biscuits and dust with icing sugar.

Make the most of your freezer

Make double the amount of custard creams, leave them unfilled and whizz to crumbs in a food processor. Freeze the crumbs to use later as the base for Chocolate orange tiffin (see page 96) or other refrigerator cakes.

Honeybuns

Midnight cookies

makes: 12 cookies
health: gluten-free
cook: 13–15 minutes
store: 7 days in airtight container. Freeze well
compost: eggshell

- 1 egg
- 150 g/5½ oz gluten-free oat flour
- 125 g/4½ oz/generous ½ cup butter, chilled and grated
- 115g/4 oz/generous ½ cup granulated sugar
- 115g/4 oz/scant 1½ cups gluten-free oats
- 1 tbsp good-quality orange marmalade
- 1 tsp gluten-free baking powder
- 1 tsp vanilla extract
- pinch of salt
- finely grated zest of 1 orange
- 115g/4 oz dark chocolate, cut into chunks
- tapioca flour, for dusting

TOPPING

- 150 g/5½ oz dark chocolate, chopped
- 1 tbsp olive oil

In the early days of Honeybuns we often spent long days and nights working in the bakery. These delicious dark chocolate and orange cookies, together with extra-shot lattes, helped to see us through.

Preheat the oven to 180°C/350°F/Gas 4. Cut a piece of baking parchment to line a large baking sheet.

Put the egg, oat flour, butter, sugar, oats, marmalade, baking powder, vanilla, salt and orange zest into a large mixing bowl and beat using an electric mixer at low speed until they start to clump together. Using a rubber spatula, stir in the chocolate chunks.

Dust your hands and work surface liberally with tapioca flour. Divide the dough into 12 equal portions (it is very sticky, so you may need to use a tablespoon). Roll into balls and place on the baking sheet. The cookies will spread as they bake, so make sure you leave plenty of space between them. Using the palms of your hands, squash each cookie into a disc about 1 cm/½ in thick.

Bake for 13–15 minutes, until light golden on top and mid-golden underneath: use a fish slice to check the bottom of a cookie after 13 minutes. Leave on the baking sheet for 5–10 minutes, then transfer to a cooling rack.

For the topping, melt the chocolate with the olive oil in a heatproof bowl set over a saucepan of gently simmering water, stirring until smooth (or in a microwave). Half dip each cookie in the melted chocolate, place on a piece of baking parchment and leave until set.

For extra 'ooh-la-la'

For a special decoration, top with roasted orange pieces (see page 102).

Iced gems

SHORTBREAD

140 g/5 oz/generous ½ cup butter, chilled and cubed
60 g/2¼ oz/½ cup icing (confectioners') sugar
60 g/2¼ oz/scant ½ cup cornflour (cornstarch)
60 g/2¼ oz/⅔ cup ground almonds
40 g/1½ oz sorghum flour
20 g/¾ oz/2 tbsp brown rice flour
tapioca flour, for dusting

TO DECORATE

25 g/1 oz raspberries
juice of 1 lemon
250–300 g/9–10½ oz royal icing (confectioners') sugar, sifted
25 g/1 oz blackcurrants
dried lavender flowers and rose petals (you can get them from www.meadowsweetflowers.co.uk)

These little delectable bites look and taste heavenly. The shortbread bases are truly melt-in-the-mouth. We have celebrated many a girly get-together with these gems, plus our bourbon and custard creams, arrayed on vintage cake stands.

Preheat the oven to 170°C/325°F/Gas 3. Cut a piece of baking parchment to line a large baking sheet.

Put the butter, icing sugar, cornflour, ground almonds, sorghum flour and rice flour into a food processor and whizz to form a soft, pliable dough. Wrap the dough in clingfilm (plastic wrap) and chill in the fridge for 30 minutes.

Dust your hands, rolling pin and work surface liberally with tapioca flour. Roll out the dough to a little over 1 cm/½ in thick. Dip a 4 cm/1½ in pastry cutter in tapioca flour and then use it to cut the dough. Place the shapes on the baking sheet. The gems will spread as they bake, so make sure you leave plenty of space between them.

Bake for 7–8 minutes, until slightly golden on the edges. Leave on the baking sheet for 5–10 minutes, then transfer to a cooling rack.

To decorate, we suggest making 2 beautifully coloured natural icings:

Press the raspberries through a fine sieve to collect the juice in a bowl; you'll get maximum juice if you microwave them on full power for 30 seconds first. Discard the pips. Add the juice from ½ lemon and then stir in about 125 g/4½ oz sifted royal icing sugar. Mix until you have a fairly stiff icing.

In a separate bowl, repeat the process with the blackcurrants.

Using a piping bag with a small star nozzle, pipe little swirls and stars onto the shortbread bases. Decorate with lavender flowers and rose petals before the icing sets too hard.

Baking tip

When baked, these biscuits will have a slightly uneven edge. For a sharper edge, bake the rolled dough in 1 piece for 8–10 minutes, leave to cool slightly, then cut out the desired shapes with a cookie cutter.

makes: 40–50 x 4 cm/1½ in gems
health: gluten-free
cook: 7–8 minutes
store: 7 days in airtight container. Freeze well
compost: bits of fruit

puddings

Fuzzy peach pudding

makes: 1 x 23 cm/9 in round tart
health: gluten-free, dairy-free
cook: 40 minutes
store: best eaten on same day
compost: eggshells

AMONDI CRUST

3 tbsp almond oil, plus extra for brushing
85 g/3 oz tapioca flour, plus extra for dusting
250 g/9 oz Amondi cookies (about 4 cookies), (see page 130)
1 egg
1 egg yolk, beaten

ROASTED PEACHES

4 peaches, pitted and each cut into 8 pieces
5 tbsp clear honey
finely grated zest and juice of 1 unwaxed lemon
1–2 tbsp cinnamon sugar

MERINGUE TOPPING

3 egg whites
1 tsp vanilla extract
85 g/3 oz/scant ½ cup granulated sugar
1–2 tbsp whole (skin-on) almonds, or hazelnuts, or both

Feel free to plunder the fruit bowl for this recipe: nectarines, plums or pears would work just as well as peaches.

Preheat the oven to 180°C/350°F/Gas 4. Brush a 23 cm/9 in round loose-bottomed tart tin with almond oil and dust with tapioca flour.

Blitz the Amondi cookies to crumbs in a food processor. Add the almond oil, egg and tapioca flour and blitz again, to form a soft pliable dough.

Dust your hands and work surface liberally with tapioca flour, then knead the dough briefly and form it into a ball. Roll in out to line the tin and press firmly over the base and a little up the sides of the tin. Don't worry about it being a bit bumpy. Bake for 10 minutes, until golden brown. Brush with beaten egg yolk and return to the oven for a further 2 minutes. Put the tin on a rack and leave to cool.

For the roasted peaches, put the peach pieces into a roasting tin with the honey and lemon zest and juice. Mix to coat the peaches and then dredge liberally with cinnamon sugar. Bake for 20 minutes, until they start to bubble. Drain the peaches in a sieve and collect the juices; set aside. Whizz half the roasted peaches in a food processor to make a purée. Spread this purée over the Amondi crust in the tart tin. Spread the remaining roasted peach pieces over the purée.

For the meringue topping, in a clean, large bowl whisk the egg whites until they form stiff peaks. Add the vanilla, then whisk in the sugar a little at a time, until the egg whites are stiff and glossy.

Spoon the meringue over the peaches – we like rustic-looking rough peaks. Scatter with whole almonds and bake for 10 minutes. The meringue peaks will be a light chestnut colour when cooked. To serve, drizzle the reserved peach juice over the pudding.

More dishes with an Amondi cookie base

Make several tart cases to keep in the freezer. Use this base mixture for Blackcurrant flummery pie (page 158) or Double chocolate and raspberry tartlets (page 106), or for a topping designed by you.

High days and holidays trifles

250 g/9 oz Amondi cookies (see page 130), broken into chunks
150 g/5½ oz Chocolate, hazelnut and cranberry cake (see page 42), broken into chunks
1 tbsp amaretto liqueur
150 g/5½ oz/generous 1 cup raspberries
150 g/5½ oz/1 cup strawberries, quartered
200 ml/7 fl oz/scant 1 cup double (heavy) cream
100 g/3½ oz dark chocolate
8 natural colour glacé (candied) cherries

ROASTED FRUITS

1 large peach, pitted and cut into 8 pieces
2 apricots, pitted and quartered
juice of ½ lime
3 tbsp clear honey
1 tbsp light brown sugar

RASPBERRY COULIS

150 g/5½ oz/generous 1 cup raspberries
2 tbsp icing (confectioners') sugar, sifted
juice of ½ lime

CUSTARD

10 egg yolks
150 g/5 oz/¾ cup caster (superfine) sugar
1 vanilla pod, seeds scraped
568 ml/1 pint whole milk
2 tsp cornflour (cornstarch)

makes: 8 individual trifles
health: gluten-free
cook: 20 minutes
store: 2 days in fridge
compost: eggshells and strawberry stalks

This looks like a blast from the 1970s, but appearances can be deceptive. We have reinterpreted this classic: the generous amount of fruit and a measure of amaretto take it to another level. It's also well worth making your own custard. Tasty sophistication in retro fancy dress.

Preheat the oven to 180°C/350°F/Gas 4. For the roasted fruits, put the peach and apricot pieces into a roasting tin with the lime juice, honey and brown sugar. Mix to coat the pieces. Bake for 20 minutes, until they start to bubble. Drain the fruit in a sieve and collect the juice; set both aside and leave to cool.

For the raspberry coulis, squash the raspberries with the icing sugar and lime juice, then push through a sieve using the back of a spoon. Discard the seeds and pulp. Taste the coulis and add more icing sugar if you like, but it should be fairly tart.

For the custard, put the egg yolks into a bowl with the sugar and seeds from the vanilla pod. Beat until thick and creamy. Warm the milk gently, until just about to boil. Remove from the heat and gradually beat into the yolk-and-sugar mixture using a hand whisk, to prevent lumps forming. You need a thick custard, so you may need to add cornflour: mix the cornflour with a little water to make a smooth paste. Return the custard to the heat, stir in as much of the cornflour paste as you need and simmer gently for 1 minute. Set aside to cool, then cover and chill in the fridge.

To assemble the trifles: divide the broken-up cookies and cake between 8 individual trifle dishes and sprinkle with the amaretto. Spoon in the roasted fruit, raspberries and strawberries, then pour the cooking syrup from the roasted fruit over the top. Divide about 6 tbsp of the raspberry coulis between the trifles and then pour 500 ml/18 fl oz/heaping 2 cups of the custard over.

Whisk the cream until it forms soft peaks, then spoon it over the custard. Grate the chocolate over the cream. Finally, pop a red cherry in the middle of each trifle.

Make the most of your freezer

Make Amondi cookies and Chocolate, hazelnut and cranberry cake ahead of time and store in the freezer – or use any type of leftover or frozen cake and cookies.

Peach and apricot custard tart

PASTRY

40 g/1½ oz/3 tbsp butter, chilled and cubed, plus extra, melted, for brushing
60 g/2¼ oz/¾ cup walnuts, ground
35 g/1¼ oz/5 tbsp icing (confectioners') sugar
25 g/1 oz sorghum flour
25 g/1 oz tapioca flour, plus extra for dusting
½ tsp gluten-free baking powder
1 small egg yolk
⅓ tsp vanilla extract
2–4 tsp whole milk
1 tbsp clear honey, for brushing
1 tbsp brown vanilla sugar, for sprinkling

ROASTED PEACH AND APRICOT FILLING

2 apricots, pitted and quartered
2 peaches, pitted and cut into 8 pieces
3 tbsp clear honey
juice of 1 lemon

CUSTARD

1 egg, plus 1 yolk
25 g/1 oz/2 tbsp caster (superfine) sugar
150 ml/5 fl oz/⅔ cup double (heavy) cream

makes: 1 x 23 cm/9 in round tart
health: gluten-free
cook: 45–50 minutes
store: 3 days in fridge. Freezes well
compost: eggshells, fruit trimmings

This tart looks and tastes like summer; it's perfect for alfresco dining. If you use soft fruits such as berries, you don't need to bake them first.

Whizz the butter, walnuts, icing sugar, sorghum flour, tapioca flour and baking powder in a food processor to form clumpy crumbs. Add the egg yolk and vanilla, then add the milk a little at a time and whizz again until you have a smooth dough (you may not need all the milk). Wrap the dough in clingfilm (plastic wrap) and chill for 1 hour.

Preheat the oven to 180°C/350°F/Gas 4. Brush a 23 cm/9 in round loose-bottomed tart tin with melted butter and line with baking parchment. Dust your hands and work surface liberally with tapioca flour, knead the dough briefly, and then form it into a ball. Put it into the tin and press firmly over the base and up the sides. Prick all over with a fork and bake for 16–18 minutes, until golden brown and firm to the touch. Warm the honey and brush it over the pastry case, then leave to cool.

For the filling, put the apricot and peach pieces into a roasting tin with the honey and lemon juice. Mix to coat the fruit. Bake for 20 minutes, until the fruit mixture starts to bubble. Drain the fruit in a sieve and collect the juices; set aside.

For the custard, put the egg and egg yolk in a bowl with the sugar. Beat until thick and creamy. Warm the cream gently in a saucepan until just about to boil. Remove from the heat and gradually beat into the yolk-and-sugar mixture using a hand whisk to prevent lumps forming. Set aside.

Arrange the baked fruit in the pastry case, then pour the fruit cooking syrup over the top. Pour the custard over the fruit until it reaches the top of the pastry case, and sprinkle with brown vanilla sugar. Bake for 10–12 minutes, until the custard is set and light golden, but still slightly wobbly. Leave in the tin to cool, then carefully lift it onto a serving plate.

For extra 'ooh-la-la'

Whisk 1 tbsp amaretto liqueur – or a drop or 2 of vanilla extract – with some crème fraîche to serve with this pud.

Strawberry cobbler

makes: 1 x 23 cm/9 in tart
health: gluten-free
cook: 30–32 minutes
store: 3 days in fridge. Freezes well
compost: eggshells

SHORTBREAD BASE

100 g/3½ oz/½ cup butter, chilled and grated, plus extra, melted, for brushing
50 g/1¾ oz/scant ½ cup icing (confectioners') sugar
50 g/1¾ oz/⅓ cup cornflour (cornstarch)
25 g/1 oz sorghum flour
15 g/½ oz/1½ tbsp brown rice flour
50 g/2 oz/½ cup ground almonds
½ tbsp whole milk (optional)
tapioca flour, for dusting
1 egg yolk, beaten
8–9 tbsp strawberry jam (with chunky fruit pieces)

COBBLER TOPPING

125 g/4½ oz/1¼ cups ground almonds
15 g/½ oz tapioca flour, plus extra for dusting
20 g/¾ oz/1½ tbsp light brown sugar
¾ tsp gluten-free baking powder
½ tsp baking soda
pinch of salt
1 egg
1 tbsp almond oil
½ tsp vanilla extract
1–2 tbsp whole milk, for brushing
1–2 tbsp brown vanilla sugar, for sprinkling

This recipe came about by happy accident. We had some leftover shortbread mix and, that same day, I'd also finished the recipe for our sweet scones. It seemed like a brilliant idea to combine the two.

Brush a 23 cm/9 in round loose-bottomed tart tin with melted butter.

To make the shortbread base, whizz the butter, sugar, cornflour, sorghum flour, rice flour and almonds in a food processor until you have a soft dough. You may need ½ tbsp milk at this stage to help it come together. If the mixture is very sticky, add a little tapioca flour, 1 tsp at a time. Wrap the dough in clingfilm and chill in the fridge for 1 hour. Preheat the oven to 180°C/350°F/Gas 4.

Dust your hands and work surface liberally with tapioca flour. Knead the dough briefly, then put it into the tin and press firmly over the base and up the sides.

Prick the shortbread several times with a fork. Bake for 15 minutes. Brush with beaten egg yolk and return to the oven for a further 2 minutes. Put the tin on a rack and leave to cool. Spread the strawberry jam over the shortbread.

For the cobbler topping, whizz the almonds, tapioca flour, light brown sugar, baking powder, baking soda and salt in a food processor. Add the egg, almond oil and vanilla and whizz until you have a soft sticky dough.

Dust your hands and work surface liberally with tapioca flour. Knead the dough briefly, then flatten it to about 5 mm/¼ in thick. Mould it into a heart shape and place it on top of the jam (it should not completely cover the jam). Brush the heart with milk and sprinkle with brown vanilla sugar, then bake for 12–15 minutes, until golden brown.

Black Forest gâteau

200 g/7 oz/scant 1 cup butter, plus extra, melted, for brushing
tapioca flour, for dusting
150 g/5½ oz dark chocolate, chopped
3 eggs
200 g/7 oz/1 cup granulated sugar
100 g/3½ oz/1 cup ground almonds
100 g/3½ oz/1¼ cups hazelnuts, ground
50 g/1¾ oz/5 tbsp ground brown flax seeds (linseed)
250 g/9 oz gluten-free black cherry compote
pinch of salt

TOPPING

100 ml/3½/⅓ cup fl oz double (heavy) cream
125 g/4½ oz crème fraîche
1 tsp vanilla extract
250 g/9 oz gluten-free black cherry compote

makes: 1 x 23 cm/9 in round cake
health: gluten-free
cook: 30 minutes
store: 3 days in fridge. Freezes well
compost: eggshells

As a child in the 1970s, I remember seeing adverts for frozen Black Forest gâteau in my mum's magazines, but the shop-bought version I finally got to try was watery and I never quite recovered from the disappointment. The only thing for it was to devise my own version, bursting with black cherry fabulousness in every mouthful.

Preheat the oven to 180°C/350°F/Gas 4. Line a 23 cm/9 in round springform tin with a disc of baking parchment, then brush with melted butter and dust with tapioca flour.

Melt the dark chocolate with the butter in a heatproof bowl set over a saucepan of gently simmering water, stirring until smooth (or in a microwave).

Crack the eggs into a mixing bowl, add the sugar, almonds, hazelnuts, flax seeds, cherry compote and salt, then pour in the melted chocolate-and-butter mixture. Beat with an electric mixer at medium-high speed until is thick and smooth.

Spoon the mixture into the tin and bang the tin firmly on a work surface to get rid of air pockets. Bake for 25 minutes, then cover with a disc of baking parchment and bake for a further 5 minutes. The cake will feel quite soft to the touch, but a flat cake skewer will come out clean when the cake is ready. Leave to cool in the tin for 5–10 minutes.

Carefully loosen the sides of the cake and remove from the tin. Place on a rack until completely cool.

For the topping, whisk the cream with the crème fraîche and vanilla using an electric mixer at high speed until stiff peaks form. Using a piping bag fitted with a star nozzle, pipe large swirls of the cream mixture around the edge of the cake. Spoon the cherry compote onto the top.

Give it a twist

The sponge, drizzled with a little melted chocolate, makes a delicious cake without the cream topping.

Scrumdiddleyumptious blueberry flan

serves: 8
health: gluten-free
cooking time: 8–10 minutes
store: best eaten on same day. Bases freeze well
compost: eggshells

- 600 g/1 lb 5 oz Scrumdiddleyumptious cookie dough (see page 129)
- 400 ml/14 fl oz/1¾ cups double (heavy) cream
- 200 g/7 oz/scant 1 cup cream cheese
- 9 tbsp lemon curd
- 400 g/14 oz/2¾ cups blueberries
- finely grated zest of 1 unwaxed lemon
- 2 tbsp clear honey

This fab dessert lends itself to any soft summer berries. The discs of Scrumdiddleyumptious will be crisp on the outside and soft and chewy on the inside. If you prefer, you could bake the mixture as 24 small discs to make individual pudding stacks. Either way, this is quick to make, pretty and delicious. The Scrumdiddleyumptious cookies recipe makes about twice what you need for this dessert, so you could either make some cookies, or freeze the spare mixture and cook it later.

Preheat the oven to 180°C/350°F/Gas 4. Cut rectangles of baking parchment big enough to line the bottoms of 3 large baking sheets, plus an extra piece.

Divide the Scrumdiddleyumptious dough into 3 equal pieces. Place the first piece in the centre of a sheet of baking parchment and cover with another sheet of parchment. Using a rolling pin, roll the dough into a disc about 5 mm/¼ in thick. Carefully peel off the top sheet of parchment and slide the bottom sheet with the dough onto a baking sheet. Repeat to make 2 more discs on parchment, and set on baking sheets.

Bake for 8–10 minutes, until golden and firm to the touch; lift the parchment to check that the underside is also golden brown. Allow to cool.

Assemble this just before serving, to prevent the discs from becoming soggy. Whisk the cream and cream cheese together until stiff peaks form.

Place a Scrumdiddleyumptious disc on a serving plate, spread over 3 tbsp of lemon curd, then one-third of the cream mixture, then sprinkle on one-third of the blueberries. Repeat with the remaining 2 discs, creating a 3-tiered dessert.

Sprinkle the zest over the top layer of blueberries and drizzle the honey over.

Give it a twist

Try drizzling maple syrup instead of honey over the top.

Baked apples en croute

serves: 4
health: gluten-free
cook: 32 minutes
store: 3 days in fridge; can be reheated
compost: eggshells, apple trimmings

4 cooking apples
150 g/5½ oz/scant 1 cup raisins
5 tbsp light brown sugar
2 tbsp Calvados or apple juice

PASTRY

140 g/5 oz/scant 1 cup brown rice flour
140 g/5 oz gluten-free oat flour
100 g/3½ oz/½ cup caster (superfine) sugar
85 g/3 oz/6 tbsp butter, chilled and grated
50 g/1¾ oz/⅔ cup hazelnuts, ground
50 g/1¾ oz vegetarian gluten-free suet
pinch of salt
2 egg yolks
2-3 tbsp whole milk
tapioca flour, for dusting

Here's our take on apple dumplings. If you don't want a full pastry set of pyjamas, just top the apples with pastry lids.

To make the pastry, whizz the rice flour, oat flour, sugar, butter, hazelnuts, suet, salt and 1 egg yolk in a food processor until the mixture resembles breadcrumbs. Gradually add the milk until you have a soft dough (you may not need all of it). Wrap the dough in clingfilm and chill in the fridge for 1 hour.

Preheat the oven to 180°C/350°F/Gas 4. Line a 30 x 23 x 4 cm/12 x 9 x 1½ in baking tin with baking parchment. Wash and core the apples and place in the baking tin. Mix the raisins and 3 tbsp of the brown sugar in a bowl; pack the mixture into the centre of the apples. Drizzle the apples with the Calvados or apple juice and sprinkle with 1 tbsp of the brown sugar. Bake for 12 minutes, then leave to cool.

Dust your hands and work surface liberally with tapioca flour. Turn the pastry out onto the work surface, knead the dough briefly, then divide it into 4 equal balls. Using your fingertips, press each ball of pastry out on a work surface into a disc about 3 mm/⅛ in thick.

Place a cooked, cooled apple in the centre of each ball of pastry and gather up the sides of the pastry, moulding it around the apple. Squidge the pastry together at the top to seal completely. Put the apple dumplings into the baking tin, brush with beaten egg yolk and sprinkle with the remaining 1 tbsp brown sugar. Bake for 20 minutes, or until the pastry is cooked through and light golden brown.

Serve with home-made custard (see page 147).

For extra 'ooh-la-la'

You could go arty and cut out pastry shapes with a cookie cutter to decorate the tops of the apples before glazing with the egg yolk.

Tinker bocker glory

serves: 4 desserts
health: gluten-free
cook: 15 minutes
store: 3 days in fridge
compost: eggshell

tapioca flour, for dusting
450 g/1 lb Triple chocolate tinker dough (see page 128)
100 ml/3½ fl oz/⅓ cup double (heavy) cream
1 tbsp whisky
2 tsp instant coffee, dissolved in 2 tsp hot water
1 tsp vanilla extract
200 g/7 oz/1¾ cups raspberries
1–2 tsp cocoa powder, for dusting

We hereby present our fabulous hybrid of tiramisu, knickerbocker glory and cranachan, a Scottish dessert made with cream, whisky and raspberries. The recipe for Triple chocolate tinkers (see page 128) makes about twice the amount of dough you need for this recipe, so freeze the rest, or bake a few cookies.

Preheat the oven to 180°C/350°F/Gas 4. Cut a rectangle of baking parchment to line the bottom of a large baking sheet. Dust your hands and work surface liberally with tapioca flour and, using your hands, shape the cookie dough into a slab about 1 cm/½ in thick. Lay it on the baking sheet and bake for 15 minutes, or until golden brown and firm to the touch. Allow to cool completely.

Once cool, use a cookie cutter to cut out 12 discs to fit inside your serving glasses.

Whisk the cream until it forms firm peaks. Pour in the whisky, coffee and vanilla and whisk to combine.

Put a tablespoon of the cream mixture into 4 serving glasses. Place a cookie disc on top and push it down gently. Then lay 3 or 4 raspberries on top, followed by another tablespoon of cream, a cookie disc, and then 5 or 6 more raspberries. Lay 1 raspberry on top to finish. Dust with cocoa powder.

For extra 'ooh-la-la'

Sprinkle crumbled freeze-dried raspberries over the top for extra zing.

Blackcurrant flummery pie

makes: 1 x 23 cm/9 in round pie
health: gluten-free
cook: 20–22 minutes
store: best eaten on same day, or overnight in fridge. Freezes well
compost: eggshells, fruit trimmings

SWEET SHORTCRUST PASTRY

40 g/1½ oz/3 tbsp butter, chilled and cubed, plus extra, melted, for brushing
40 g/1½ oz/7 tbsp ground almonds
35 g/1¼ oz/5 tbsp icing (confectioners') sugar, sifted
20 g/¾ oz sorghum flour
20 g/¾ oz tapioca flour, plus extra for dusting
1 egg yolk, plus 1, beaten
½ tsp guar gum
½ tsp salt
finely grated zest of 1 orange
½ tbsp whole milk
tapioca flour, for dusting

FILLING AND TOPPING

2 egg whites
50 g/1¾ oz/¼ cup light brown sugar, plus extra for dredging
1 tsp cornflour (cornstarch)
100 g/3½ oz/scant 1 cup blackcurrants, plus a handful to finish
2 tsp lemon juice
225 g/8 oz/generous ½ cup blackcurrant jam

Our sweet shortcrust pastry is so easy to work. Although it lacks the stretch of its gluten-based cousins, you can roll this out and patch any joins together as you go; it's very forgiving. The topping can be varied according to what soft fruits you have to hand.

For the pastry, whizz the butter, almonds, icing sugar, sorghum flour, tapioca flour, 1 egg yolk, guar gum, salt and orange zest in a food processor until a soft dough is formed. Mix in the milk if necessary. Wrap the dough in clingfilm (plastic wrap) and chill in the fridge for 1 hour.

Preheat the oven to 180°C/350°F/Gas 4. Line a 23 cm/9 in loose-bottomed tart tin with a disc of baking parchment, then brush with melted butter and dust with tapioca flour.

Dust your hands, rolling pin and work surface liberally with tapioca flour, knead the dough briefly, then form it into a ball. Roll it out and use to line the tin. It's quite a delicate pastry, but don't worry if it breaks: you can use your fingers to smooth the joins together. Once in the tin, press the dough up the sides.

Prick all over with a fork and bake for 8 minutes, until golden brown and firm to the touch. Brush with beaten egg yolk and bake for a further 2 minutes. Leave to cool.

For the filling, whisk the egg whites in a large, clean bowl until they form stiff peaks. Whisk in the sugar and cornflour. Using a fork, partly crush the blackcurrants together with the lemon juice (don't demolish them entirely), until the juice is oozing. Fold the semi-crushed berries into the egg white mixture.

Spread the cooled pastry base thickly with blackcurrant jam, pushing it up the sides. Spread the egg white-and-blackcurrant mixture over the jam, and scatter a handful of blackcurrants on top. Dredge with brown sugar. Bake for 10–12 minutes, until the peaks of the topping turn golden. Serve.

Give it a twist

Use chopped strawberries (and strawberry jam) instead of blackcurrants. Sprinkle with crushed freeze-dried strawberries after baking.

Sweet tian

serves: 4–6
health: gluten-free
cook: 50–55 minutes
store: 3 days in fridge; can be reheated
compost: eggshells, fruit trimmings

Reading Elizabeth David's 'Is there a Nutmeg in the House' (Michael Joseph, 2000) one evening, I came across her savoury tian recipe. The word 'tian' refers to the traditional Provençal cooking dish used. After some tinkering, I devised this sweet version, which is rather like a posh bread and butter pudding. Great for using up any leftover sponge cakes or muffins (it doesn't matter if they are slightly stale). The coconut milk keeps it quite light – if you want extra richness you can use half coconut milk and half single (light) cream.

- 300 g/10½ oz peaches or apricots, pitted
- 2–3 tbsp clear honey
- 225 g/8 oz sweet muffins (see pages 50–57) or sponge cake, broken into chunks
- 150 ml/5 fl oz/⅔ cup canned coconut milk
- ½ tsp vanilla extract
- 3–4 tbsp cinnamon sugar
- 6 eggs
- ½ tbsp butter

Preheat the oven to 180°C/350°F/Gas 4. Slice the peaches, then put them into a roasting tin, drizzle with the honey and bake for 20 minutes. Set aside to cool, then purée in a food processor.

Put the muffin chunks into a large mixing bowl. Stir in the coconut milk, vanilla and 2–3 tbsp of the cinnamon sugar.

Beat the eggs with an electric mixer at high speed until foamy. Add the fruit purée and beat again.

Put the butter into a 20 cm/8 in diameter, 8cm/3 in deep casserole dish and place in the oven to melt. Retrieve the dish and pour in the muffin-and-coconut milk mixture. Pour the egg-and-fruit mixture over the top and dredge with the remaining cinnamon sugar. Bake for 30–35 minutes. The tian will rise and develop a golden brown skin. Serve warm.

Give it a twist

Use 150 g/5 oz dried apricots, finely chopped, dried cranberries and raisins instead of the roasted peaches. No need to purée them – just mix them with the egg.

Almond and apple crumble

500 g/1 lb 2 oz Bramley apples, peeled, cored and roughly chopped
50 g/1¾ oz/5 tbsp raisins
60 g/2 oz/5 tbsp light brown sugar
2 tbsp Somerset cider brandy or Calvados (optional)
double cream, whisked, to serve

CRUMBLE

100 g/3½ oz/¾ cup almonds, toasted and roughly chopped
55 g/2 oz/½ cup ground almonds
100 g/3½ oz/½ cup brown vanilla sugar
90 g/3¼ oz/¾ cup polenta
85 g/3 oz/6 tbsp butter, chilled and grated
1 tbsp light brown sugar, for sprinkling

A versatile and easy-to-make crumble topping. We love it with apples, as here, but you can sprinkle it over baked apples or use it with any fruits that are in season. Plums, peaches and damsons all work well with it, and once December festivities are under way, mix some mincemeat in with the fruit.

Preheat the oven to 180°C/350°F/Gas 4. Put the apples, raisins, brown sugar, cider brandy and 3 tbsp water (if not using cider brandy use an extra 2 tbsp water) into a saucepan and simmer over a medium heat, stirring regularly, for 5–10 minutes, until the apple has softened and is starting to break up.

For the crumble, put the toasted almonds, ground almonds, brown vanilla sugar, polenta and butter into a bowl and beat with an electric mixer at low speed until they start to clump together.

Put the fruit into a 18 cm/7 in diameter, 6 cm/2½ in deep round ovenproof dish. Sprinkle the crumble mixture over the top, making sure the fruit is covered. Sprinkle with the light brown sugar and bake for 25–30 minutes, until golden and quite firm. Serve with lashings of whisked cream.

serves: 4
health: gluten-free
cook: 30–40 minutes
store: 3 days in fridge. Freezes well
compost: fruit trimmings

Make the most of your freezer

Make double the amount of crumble topping and freeze half.

Peach and raspberry roulade

5 eggs, separated
140 g/5 oz/scant ¾ cup caster (superfine) sugar
60 g/2¼ oz/⅔ cup ground almonds
grated zest of 2 unwaxed lemons
juice of 1 lemon
icing (confectioners') sugar, for dusting

FILLING

300 ml/10 fl oz/1¼ cups double (heavy) cream
150 g/5½ oz/⅔ cup mascarpone cheese
1 tbsp clear honey
1 large peach, pitted and cut into about 16 cubes
200 g/7 oz/1¾ cups raspberries

serves: 8
health: gluten-free
cook: 16–18 minutes
store: best eaten on same day, or overnight in fridge. Freezes well
compost: eggshells, fruit trimmings

Marguerita is a great cook and friend. She very kindly agreed to share the recipe for this light-as-a-feather dessert, and told us, 'This is a dead easy supper party dessert and has not failed me yet.' The rolling of it takes a bit of care. It works well made with any soft fruit. Serve it on a white or cream plate, surrounded by fresh raspberries and peaches.

Preheat the oven to 180°C/350°F/Gas 4. Line a 35 x 30 cm/14 x 12 in baking tin with baking parchment.

Whisk together the egg yolks and caster sugar until pale and very thick. Whisk in the almonds and the lemon zest and juice.

In a separate large, clean bowl, whisk the egg whites until very stiff. Using a metal spoon, fold the whites into the yolk mixture and pour into the tin. Bake for 16–18 minutes, or until firm to the touch. Slide the roulade (still on the baking parchment) onto a rack, cover with a clean, damp tea-towel and leave to cool for about 2 hours.

Dust a sheet of baking parchment with icing sugar and turn the cooled roulade out upside-down onto the sugar. Peel off the parchment.

To make the filling, whisk together the cream and mascarpone until thick but not stiff. Smooth over the roulade using a palette knife, spreading it evenly to the edges. Drizzle the honey over the cream mixture.

Arrange the peach cubes and raspberries over the cream mixture and push in slightly. Then, with the longest side nearest you, use the baking parchment to roll the roulade away from you into a Swiss roll shape. Run your hands along the length of the roll to tighten it up, then roll the roulade out of the parchment and onto a serving plate. Dust with icing sugar and serve.

Make it easy

This recipe is easier if the raspberries are slightly frozen because they hold their shape better.

Chocolate, pear and hazelnut tart

makes: 1 x 23 cm/9 in round tart
health: gluten-free
cook: 40–45 minutes
store: 3 days in fridge. Freezes well
compost: eggshells, pear trimmings

PASTRY

25 g/1 oz/2 tbsp butter, plus extra, melted, for brushing
150 g/5½ oz/generous 1 cup hazelnuts, toasted and ground
25 g/1 oz/2 tbsp light brown sugar
pinch of salt
tapioca flour, for dusting

CHOCOLATE LAYER

100 g/3½ oz dark chocolate, chopped
1 tsp almond oil

POACHED PEARS

2 large pears (about 200 g/7 oz), peeled, cored and each cut lengthways into 6 pieces
2 tbsp granulated sugar

CHOCOLATE MOUSSE FILLING

60 g/2¼ oz milk chocolate, chopped
60 g/2¼ oz dark chocolate, chopped
50 g/1¾ oz/4 tbsp butter
2 eggs
100 g/3½ oz/5 tbsp rice syrup
85 g/3 oz crème fraîche
40 g/1½ oz/½ cup hazelnuts, ground

TOPPING

25 g/1 oz/3 tbsp whole hazelnuts, toasted

This tart is devilishly moreish. We've found it's good to wheel out if we're being visited by hard-nosed business chaps… one spoonful and they're putty.

Brush a 23 cm/9 in round loose-bottomed tart tin with melted butter and line with baking parchment. To make the pastry, whizz the butter, hazelnuts, sugar and salt together in a food processor until soft and clumpy. Wrap the dough in clingfilm and chill in the fridge for 1 hour. Preheat the oven to 150°C/300°F/Gas 2.

Press the pastry into the tin using the back of a metal spoon and smooth it down, almost like a biscuit base. Prick with a fork and bake for 15–18 minutes, until golden and firm. Take care not to overbake or it will crumble. Set aside to cool and turn the oven off.

Melt the dark chocolate with the almond oil in a heatproof bowl set over a saucepan of gently simmering water, stirring until smooth (or in a microwave). Stir well and spread over the cooked, cooled pastry base. Chill in the fridge for 1 hour. Preheat the oven to 180°C/350°F/Gas 4.

For the poached pears, put the pear pieces into a saucepan with the sugar and 3 tbsp water. Cook over a medium heat, stirring, for about 5 minutes, or until they are soft and cooked but keep their shape. The syrup should have reduced to coat the pears; there should be no excess liquid in the pan. Set aside to cool.

For the filling, melt the milk chocolate, dark chocolate and butter together in a heatproof bowl set over a saucepan of gently simmering water, stirring until smooth (or in a microwave). Set aside. Crack the eggs into a bowl, then add the rice syrup, crème fraîche, hazelnuts and a pinch of salt. Add the melted chocolate mixture and beat with an electric mixer at high speed until pale and fluffy.

Arrange the pears on the chocolate-coated pastry base. Pour the chocolate mousse filling over the pears to fill the case to the top. Sprinkle the whole toasted hazelnuts over the top. Bake for 16–18 minutes, until the filling has just set. Take care not to overbake – the filling should still be slightly wobbly.

For chocolate pots

To make mini chocolate pots, pour the chocolate mousse filling into buttered ramekins and bake at 170°C/325°F/Gas 3 for 20 minutes.

Ginger and lemon pudding

GINGER BISCUIT BASE

70 g/2½ oz/5 tbsp butter, plus extra, melted, for brushing

50 g/1¾ oz/5 tbsp brown rice flour

40 g/1½ oz tapioca flour, plus extra, for dusting

1 tsp ground ginger

¼ tsp gluten-free baking powder

25 g/1 oz/2 tbsp caster (superfine) sugar

½ tbsp stem ginger in syrup, drained and finely chopped

FILLING

3 tbsp ginger jam

150 ml/5 fl oz/⅔ cup double (heavy) cream

200 g/7 oz/1 cup condensed milk

finely grated zest and juice of ½ unwaxed lemon

ROASTED LEMON TOPPING

1 lemon

juice of ½ lemon

1 tbsp granulated sugar

makes: 1 x 23 cm/9 in round tart
health: gluten-free
cook: 22–24 minutes
store: 2 days in fridge. Freezes well
compost: bits of lemon

Use a good-quality ginger jam or try a ginger and fruit mix for this pud – ginger and rhubarb jam works brilliantly.

Preheat the oven to 180°C/350°F/Gas 4. Line a baking sheet with baking parchment. Brush a 23 cm/9 in round loose-bottomed tart tin with melted butter and line with baking parchment.

Whizz 50 g/1¾ oz/4 tbsp of the butter in a food processor with the rice flour, tapioca flour, ground ginger, baking powder, caster sugar and chopped ginger until a dough is formed; this can take a while. Mould with your hands if necessary when it's soft and clumpy.

Dust your hands and work-surface liberally with tapioca flour, knead the dough briefly, then put it on the baking sheet and flatten to about 5 mm/¼ in thick. Bake for 12–14 minutes, until golden and firm to the touch. Leave to cool and turn the oven off.

Blitz the cooked ginger biscuit dough to fine crumbs in a food processor. Melt the remaining 20 g/¾ oz/1 tbsp butter, add the crumbs and stir well. Press the crumb mixture firmly into the tart tin to cover the bottom and go halfway up the sides, using the back of a metal spoon. Cover and chill in the fridge for 2 hours.

For the filling, spread the ginger jam over the biscuit base. Whisk the cream in a large bowl until it forms soft peaks. Add the condensed milk and whisk until it starts to thicken. Add the lemon zest and juice and whisk again until slightly firmer than soft peaks; take care not to make it too stiff. Pour this over the biscuit base and smooth with a palette knife. Chill in the fridge for 2 hours, until set.

To make the roasted lemon topping, preheat the oven to 180°C/350°F/Gas 4. Slice the lemon into 6 rounds and place in a small non-stick baking tin. Add the lemon juice and granulated sugar, stir well and bake for 10 minutes. Baste the lemon slices in the cooking syrup and then leave to cool. Once the filling has set, arrange the lemon slices over the top.

For extra biscuits

Make double the amount of ginger biscuit base, shape into round biscuits and bake for 12–14 minutes for delicious gingersnap biscuits.

Trish's baked lemon cheesecake

makes: 1 x deep 13 cm/5 in round cheesecake
health: gluten-free
cook: 45–50 minutes
store: 3 days in fridge. Freezes well
compost: eggshell, bits of lemon

- 60 g/2¼ oz/4½ tbsp butter, melted, plus extra for brushing
- 115 g/4 oz gluten-free oatcakes
- 200 g/7 oz/scant 1 cup mascarpone cheese
- 75 g/2¾ oz/⅓ cup caster (superfine) sugar
- 50 g/1¾ oz crème fraîche
- 1 egg
- ¼ tsp vanilla extract
- finely grated zest of 2 unwaxed lemons
- juice of 1 lemon
- splash of limoncello (optional)
- 100 ml/3½ fl oz/⅓ cup double (heavy) cream

Trish has been a member of the team since we moved to Dorset, back in 2002. Supper at her cosy cottage is always a fun-filled occasion, and this baked cheesecake is her signature dessert. Best served with fresh thick cream and a dollop of good lemon curd.

Preheat the oven to 180°C/350°F/Gas 4. Brush a high-sided 13 cm/5 in diameter loose-bottomed cake tin liberally with melted butter.

Blitz the oatcakes to crumbs in a food processor. Spread over a baking sheet and bake for 5 minutes, or until golden. Remove from the oven and turn the oven off.

Mix the crumbs with the melted butter and stir well until evenly combined, then press the mixture over the base of the tin using the back of a metal spoon. Chill for 1 hour, until set. Preheat the oven to 150°C/300°F/Gas 2.

Beat the mascarpone, sugar, crème fraîche, egg, vanilla, half the lemon zest and all the juice and the limoncello, if using, with an electric mixer at medium speed until smooth. Pour the mixture over the oatcake base. Bake for 40–45 minutes. Leave to cool, then chill in the fridge for at least 2 hours, or preferably overnight.

Loosen the sides with a palette knife, then lift the cheesecake out of the tin onto a serving plate. Whisk the cream until it forms stiff peaks. Spread this carefully over the cheesecake, then sprinkle the remaining lemon zest over the top.

Give it a twist

Try oranges instead of lemons and Grand Marnier instead of limoncello.

Chocolate lime pie

makes: 1 x 23 cm/9 in round pie
health: gluten-free
cook: 42 minutes
store: 3 days in fridge.
compost: eggshells, bits of lime

CHOCOLATE BISCUIT BASE

40 g/1½ oz/3 tbsp butter, plus extra, melted, for brushing
tapioca flour, for dusting
175 g/6 oz Bourbon creams dough (see page 126)
4 tbsp lemon curd

FILLING AND TOPPING

3 egg whites
400 g/14 oz condensed milk
250 g/9 oz/1 cup ricotta cheese
1 egg
finely grated zest and juice of 4 limes
50 g/1¾ oz dark chocolate, finely grated

Chocolate limes – a crisp, tangy lime candy shell with a soft chocolate centre – were one of the sweeties we hankered after as kids. This recipe replicates the sweet as a dessert. The recipe for Bourbon creams makes enough dough for 4 pies, so you could either freeze some or make some biscuits as well.

Preheat the oven to 180°C/350°F/Gas 4. Cut a rectangle of baking parchment to line a large baking sheet. Brush a 23 cm/9 in round loose-bottomed tart tin with melted butter.

Dust your hands, rolling pin and work surface liberally with tapioca flour, knead the Bourbon creams dough briefly, then form it into a ball. Roll it out to about 5 mm/¼ in thick. Place it on the baking sheet and bake for 12 minutes, until mid-brown and firm to the touch. Leave to cool completely.

Blitz the cooked dough to crumbs in a food processor. Melt the butter, then add the crumbs and stir well. Using the back of a metal spoon, press this mixture firmly into the tart tin.

For a smooth finish, cover the crumbs with a disc of baking parchment before pressing down with the spoon. Press the mixture right up the sides of the tin. Cover and chill in the fridge for 2 hours, until firm. Carefully spread the lemon curd over the base. Preheat the oven to 180°C/350°F/Gas 4.

For the lime filling, beat the egg whites in a large, clean bowl until they form stiff peaks. In a separate bowl, beat together the condensed milk, ricotta, egg and lime zest and juice. Fold the beaten egg whites into the condensed milk mixture. Pour the lime filling into the tart tin. Bake for 30 minutes; the topping will still be slightly wobbly when you take it from the oven. Leave to cool for at least 20 minutes. Sprinkle with finely grated dark chocolate. Cover and allow to set in the fridge for 2 hours before serving.

For extra 'ooh-la-la'

For a nostalgia trip, serve the cake surrounded by wrapped chocolate lime sweeties (from www.aquarterof.co.uk).

Spotted dick

almond oil, for brushing
5 large eggs, separated
150 g/5½ oz/¾ cup caster (superfine) sugar
100 g/3½ oz/scant 1 cup dried sour cherries (or cranberries)
85 g/3 oz/generous ¾ cup ground almonds
50 g/1¾ oz/⅔ cup hazelnuts, ground
40 g/1½ oz mixed (candied) peel
finely grated zest and juice of 1 unwaxed orange

Traditionally, a Spotted dick contains suet, but we've substituted ground nuts. Their natural oils add moistness and body and there is no need for any other fat or oil. It's a beautifully textured pudding, light yet sustaining. Dried cherries or cranberries work well with the orange zest, but you can use other dried fruits and nuts. Best served hot with lashings of home-made custard (see page 147).

Preheat the oven to 180°C/350°F/Gas 4. Brush an 18 cm/7 in round pudding basin liberally with almond oil.

Whisk the egg yolks with the sugar until pale and thick. In a separate large, clean bowl, whisk the egg whites until they form stiff peaks.

Stir the cherries, almonds, hazelnuts, mixed peel and orange zest and juice into the yolk-and-sugar mixture. Fold in the egg whites using a rubber spatula or large metal spoon, until evenly combined, taking care not to knock out the air. Pour the mixture into the pudding basin.

Bake for 30 minutes, then cover with a disc of baking parchment and cook for a further 10 minutes, until just firm to the touch but still slightly wobbly. A flat cake skewer will come out clean but moist when the pudding is ready.

Leave to cool slightly, then loosen the sides with a palette knife and turn out onto a plate. Serve with vanilla custard.

makes: 1 x 18 cm/7 in round pudding
health: gluten-free
cook: 40 minutes
store: 3 days in fridge. Freezes well
compost: eggshells, bits of orange

For a winter pud

100 g/3½ oz gluten-free mincemeat would be a seasonal addition for a winter pudding.

Gluten-free storecupboard

All of the ingredients that we use are both gluten-free and vegetarian. Where we suggest a supplier or suppliers for ingredients, either they are listed in the Coeliac UK Food and Drink Directory or we have certification from the manufacturer that the ingredient is gluten-free. Please note that certifications may change, so it is essential to check the allergen statements on the packaging before using an ingredient.

The recipes in this book are not just for people who are coeliac/gluten-intolerant. If you are not, you need not seek out oats or chocolate that have been certified gluten-free. However, naturally gluten-free ingredients, such as ground flax seed and chestnut flour, will bring fabulous flavour and texture to your baking.

Ale
Glebe Farm's Gladiator (and Pathfinder) gluten-free ale(s) is available from www.glebe-farm-shop.co.uk

Baking powder
Doves Farm and Pure gluten-free baking powders are available from supermarkets and online.

Cheese
Blue cheese may have a mould that was started on bread, so may not be certified gluten-free. We use Dorset Blue Vinny from Woodbridge Farm, which is certified gluten-free (dorsetblue.moonfruit.com).

Chestnut flour
Chestnut flour has a natural sweetness and nutty flavour. It works particularly well in dense, chocolatey cakes. It's available from larger supermarkets and specialist food shops, and online.

Chickpea flour (gram flour)
We use this sparingly, as it can leave a slightly bitter aftertaste. However, it's great blended with other flours in savoury pastries. Readily available online and from Asian food stores.

Chocolate
Most chocolate isn't certified gluten-free, because the majority of manufacturers process cereals on the same site, for example for making biscuits or wafers. Labels on chocolate typically say 'may contain traces of cereal'.

We use white, milk (35 per cent cocoa solids) and dark (73 per cent cocoa solids) chocolate, in the form of callets (chocolate drops or discs), which melt easily and don't need to be chopped. They are made by a company called Barry Callebaut and are gluten-free; the dark chocolate is also dairy-free. Callebaut chocolate is popular among chefs and chocolatiers. It is not available on the high street: we get ours from HB Ingredients (you can find them at www.hbingredients.co.uk – the callets are listed as Easimelt). If you feel that the Barry Callebaut packs are too large, then Kinnerton gluten-free and dairy-free chocolate bars are available in most supermarkets and online (www.kinnerton.com).

Coconut chips
Raw unsweetened coconut chips are available online. You can substitute desiccated coconut.

Coconut flour
Coconut flour has a dominant flavour, which works well where you want a coconut flavour, but it's not generally interchangeable with other flours.

Confectionery
Sweets and chocolate confectionery may be subject to contamination at the manufacturers', but gluten-free confectionery is increasingly available at supermarkets. One of our recipes calls for wrapped chocolate lime sweeties, which are available from:
sweetgreetingsshildon.co.uk – they ship worldwide.

Cornflakes (gluten-free)
Many supermarkets sell own-label gluten-free cornflakes.

Cornflour (cornstarch)
Cornflour is great in shortbreads as it lends a 'melt-in-the-mouth' quality. Best used blended with other flours, as it hasn't enough body to be used on its own.

Flaxseed (brown, ground) (linseed)
We love the nutty, sweet flavour and high moisture content of this flour. It is often interchangeable with sorghum, millet and gluten-free oat flours. Prewett's brand is available from health food shops and from some supermarkets 'free from' ranges, or online.

Guar gum
For binding and thickening we use guar gum, a natural product made from a type of bean. We prefer guar gum to xanthan gum, which we find can result in a slightly heavier texture in some recipes.

Hazelnut flour
Bob's Red Mill hazelnut meal flour is available online. Alternatively, you can toast and grind your own nuts.

Jams, compotes, curds and butters
Jams, conserves and marmalades are naturally gluten-free. Lemon curd, mincemeat and peanut butters may be gluten-free – check the label. We suggest using your local suppliers, for example producers at a farmers' market will be able to advise you whether a product is gluten-free.

Millet flakes
Big Oz organic millet flakes are available from various online suppliers.

Millet flour
Allergycare millet flour is available from various online suppliers.

Oats and oat flour
We have included gluten-free oats and gluten-free oat flour in some recipes. These can be difficult to source due to possible contamination from wheat or other cereals in the field or mill – and some coeliacs are sensitive even to pure oats. For more information see www.coeliac.org.uk/gluten-free-diet-lifestyle/the-gluten-free-diet/what-about-oats.

Bob's Red Mill is a range of gluten-free flours and cereals. Millet flour and millet flakes are a good alternative if you'd prefer to avoid oats.

Oatcakes
Nairn's oatcakes, available from shops and supermarkets, are gluten-free.

Polenta
For baking, we use dry, finely ground polenta (not the pre-cooked blocks). It's great combined with other flours or ground nuts. In our shortbread base (page 82)

we mix it with ground almonds. Merchant Gourmet and Natco polenta are readily available.

Quinoa flour
Available online and in some health food shops.

Rice crispies (gluten-free)
Barkat gluten-free rice crunchies are available online. Some supermarkets have their own-label gluten-free rice crispies.

Rice flour
Brown rice flour is available online and in some health food shops and supermarkets. Glutinous rice flour is also gluten-free: 'glutinous' refers to the stickiness of the rice. Available from Asian food stores and online from www.thai-food-online.co.uk.

Rice syrup
Biona and Crazy Jack brands are available online.

Sausages
We recommend The Somerset Sausage Company (www.thesomersetsausagecompany.co.uk) for gluten-free vegetarian sausages.

Sorghum flour (juwar)
This fabulous flour produces a lovely fluffy cake texture and can be used blended or on its own. Available from Asian food stores, or online from: www.jalpurmillersonline.com.

Soya mince (dried, gluten-free)
Granose dried gluten-free soya mince is available from supermarkets and health food shops.

Suet
Gluten-free vegetarian suet is available from supermarkets and online.

Tapioca flour (cassava flour)
Tapioca flour is similar to cornflour (cornstarch): it's very soft and neutral in flavour. Best used blended with other flours. Infinity Foods brand is available in health food shops and online.

Worcestershire sauce
Life Free From vegan gluten-free Worcestershire sauce is available from supermarkets. In the UK and Canada, Lea & Perrins Worcestershire sauce contains malt vinegar, and thus is not gluten-free. However, Coeliac UK says Barley malt vinegar is made using a fermentation process and the end product only contains a trace amount of gluten, well below the level which is safe for most people with coeliac disease.

Dairy-free ingredients

Butter
Butter substitutes such as 'Pure' dairy-free spread are available in some supermarkets and health food stores.

Chocolate
Dark chocolate should be dairy-free, but some manufacturers use the same production line for their milk chocolate products. In dairy-free recipes we use 73 per cent dark chocolate in block form from Barry Callebaut (see page 170), which is certified dairy-free.

Cream
Cream substitutes are readily available in shops and supermarkets.

Cheese

Parmazano is a good dairy-free, vegan and gluten-free alternative to Parmesan. and is available from supermarkets. Soya-based cheese alternatives can be found in health food shops and supermarkets. We like 'Sheese' cream cheese by Bute Island Foods (buteisland.com); the range also includes Cheddar-style, mozzarella-style and other hard cheese.

Pesto

Meridian dairy-free, gluten-free green pesto is available from goodnessdirect.co.uk and naturallygoodfood.co.uk.

Other ingredients

Egg white

Egg white in pasteurized liquid form is sold in many supermarkets.

Flowers

For decorating cakes, cookies and desserts we often used dried or crystallized flowers from:
www.meadowsweetflowers.co.uk.

Fruit

Support your local pick-your-own farms: the following website covers many countries and will help you find a fruit farm; it also gives tips on how to preserve the fruit:
www.pickyourownfarms.org.uk.

Hazelnut syrup

We use Monin brand syrup, available from food shops and some supermarkets or from nextdaycoffee.co.uk.

Natural colour glacé (candied) cherries

Natural colour, glacé cherries are available from some supermarkets and online.

Oils

KTC almond oil is available from Indian groceries, such as nivala.co.uk. Boyajian oils (including lemon, orange, basil and garlic) are available from finefoodspecialist.co.uk. Almond oil is lovely, sweet and not overpowering, but quite pricey. Corn or vegetable oil can be substituted if you prefer.

Raspberries (freeze-dried) – you can get them from healthysupplies.co.uk. Freeze-dried raspberries are expensive and they soften once crushed and exposed to the air. To keep them in tip-top condition, store them in an air-tight tin and crumble them as you need them.

Additional online suppliers

Many of these online retailers sell a wide range of health foods and allergen-free foods:

goodnessdirect.co.uk
greenlife.co.uk
healthreaction.com
healthysupplies.co.uk
herbsgardenshealth.co.uk
innovative-solutions.org.uk
justingredients.co.uk
prewetts.co.uk

Index

thank yous

It has been heart-warming to reflect on everyone's generosity of spirit whilst working together on our book. Thank you so very much.

Matt and Winnie made home a lovely place to be during those intense 'Booky' months.

Charlotte Drake-Smith – your talent, loyalty and friendship underpin this whole project – and Honeybuns as a whole.

Audrey, for looking after the little scamp.

Fantastic food photography, magically created by Cristian and Roy (www.crisbarnett.com).

The Honeybuns team (including a couple of honoraries), who helped with everything from recipe testing to keeping us calm (most of the time): Charlotte, Matt, George, Jan, Lottie, Sheila, Ali, Sally, Sharon, Vicky, Elaine, Nicky, Dan, Georgia, Aaron, Victoria, Colin, Os, Lorraine, Myra, Graham, Barry, Jenny, Jasmine, Nina, Veebee, Laura, Tess, Gay, Trish, Marguerita and Honey.

Brilliant design support from Sara and Moira at Stable Design (www.stabledesign.co.uk) and our own Graham Goodger, particularly for the **Honeybuns font**

Creative gurus and generous prop-lending friends Beverley and Lance of the Muddy Dog Company (www.muddydogs.com).

Dr Andrew Pannifer for his knowledge of West Country apple varieties.

Sally's crew of tireless recipe testers: Nick and the uber-tastic Sally, John, Jackie, Maggie and Nick, Yvonne, Louise, Carole, Lucy, Katie and Dick.

The Anova publishing team, particularly Becca Spry for keeping us in line, Kom for being so helpful and Polly for finding us in the first place.

The little people who came to the party in some of the photos: Alex, Flissy, Henry, Niamh, Bella, Gabriel, Ella and Winston.

Sally Drake, Kelly and Daisy for props. Edward Oliver for the kind loan of your vintage fridge (www.edward-oliver.co.uk). Susan Young (www.alwestonjamandchutney.co.uk), UK's National Jampion 2011. Oxford's Bakery for supplying us with lovely lunch provisions (www.oxfordsbakery.co.uk). Holwell Village Hall Committee for your kind loan of the hallowed Hall.

Kindly neighbours and friends in Holwell for your support – in particular the Moormead posse, Aud, Jo 'n' Jack, Maurice and Caroline, Neil and Alison and the Joneses.